The Fine Art of Success

The Fine Art of Success

How Learning Great Art Can Create Great Business

Jamie Anderson, Jörg Reckhenrich
and
Martin Kupp

John Wiley & Sons, Inc.

Library of Congress Cataloging-in-Publication Data
Anderson, Jamie, 1971-
    The fine art of success : how learning great art can create great business / by Jamie Anderson, Jörg Reckhenrich, and Martin Kupp.
        p. cm.
    Includes bibliographical references and index.
    ISBN 978-0-470-66106-2 (cloth : alk. paper)   1.   Creative ability in business.
    2.   Marketing.   3.   Success in business.   I. Reckhenrich, Jörg.   II. Kupp, Martin.
III. Title.
    HD53.A48 2011
    658.4'09–dc22   2010045342

A catalogue record for this book is available from the British Library.

All drawings and images are courtesy of Jörg Reckhenrich

ISBN 978-0-470-66106-2 (hardback), ISBN 978-1-119-99016-1 (ebk),
ISBN 978-1-119-99253-0 (ebk), ISBN 978-1-119-99254-7 (ebk)

Typeset in 9.5/13pt Melior by Thomson Digital, Noida, India
Printed in Great Britain by TJ International Ltd, Padstow, Cornwall, UK

Dedication

To my parents, Lee and Valerie Jean. You instilled in me a passion for life, and the joy of giving.

Jamie L. Anderson

To my wife Claudia. You always believed and shared in what I have dreamed of.

Jörg Reckhenrich

To my family and best friends, Ilona, Mats, Hanne and Ida, who inspire me and make my life purposeful.

Martin Kupp

Contents

Foreword

Costas Markides, London Business School

Creativity is enhanced when we approach a task from different angles. For example, I once observed a colleague teach a group of business executives how to make their companies more innovative. He first asked them to identify other companies that are known for their innovativeness and consider how they achieved it. But once they'd had a long discussion on what other companies did to promote innovation, he then asked his audience to forget business organizations and compare, instead, the difference between capitalism and communism as economic systems. What is it about the capitalist system that allowed it to prosper and win the economic war against capitalism? Which of these characteristics of capitalism can we import into our companies? Once they had debated on this topic, he asked them to think about their families. What did they do at home to encourage their children to develop their creativity? And how many of these tactics can be transferred into their companies?

In the process of looking at innovation from three different angles – what other companies do; why did capitalism win; what do you do at home – the executives were able to develop a wealth of ideas on how to promote innovation in their companies. With each different angle of approaching the task, they generated more and different ideas. Variety in how they approached the task produced variety in the end result.

This book is a wonderful application of this principle. The business topics covered are well-known to business managers – how to rejuvenate one's strategy; how to strategically innovate and create new market space; how to globalize; how to become more creative. A lot has been written about these topics but few authors have approached them from the perspective of the arts. This book fills this void. In doing so, it achieves two major objectives: (a) it allows the reader to approach the task (such as how to innovate or how to globalize) from a totally different angle, something that produces surprising new insights; and (b) it allows us to discuss these mundane business issues in an entertaining fashion through interesting stories from the arts world.

Take, for example, the chapter on Madonna. It is obvious that Madonna did not base her success on luck or talent alone. Instead, she thought carefully about her market and customers as well as her own unique competences and aspirations to develop a differentiated personal strategy. But even before her successful strategy had run its course, Madonna was brave enough to challenge it and change it. Rather than wait until a crisis hit her, Madonna did what we all teach our executives to do – dare to change when times are good, not when you face a crisis. This chapter describes how exactly she did this. The analysis of what she did and how she did it provides numerous insights to practicing managers.

In exploring important business topics through the eyes of the art world, this book also shatters one of the most damaging myths that managers hold dear to their hearts – that *their* situation is unique and that the pressures *they* are under in today's world are unparalleled. As story after story in this book demonstrates, this could not be further from the truth! The world was as fast-changing and demanding 500 years ago as it is today; and five centuries ago, people faced the same challenges – how to strategically innovate; how to create new market space; how to globalize – that managers of today do.

Take for example the topic of strategic innovation. In recent years, it's become popular to call for companies to break the rules in their industries in order to create new market space. By this, people mean that companies ought to search for new customer segments, new value propositions and new ways of delivering value to customers. Yet, as the chapter on Damien Hirst demonstrates, this is exactly what he did to create new market space in the art market. And as the chapter on Tintoretto shows, the concept of strategic innovation has deep historical roots that go all the way back to 16th Century Venice.

The final contribution of the book lies in the way it delivers its messages. We know that story-telling is an effective way of communicating messages and inspiring people. This is what we do every time we tell a bedtime story to our children and it's a technique that we use abundantly in the classroom. Leaders – in politics or business – also know the importance of stories in galvanizing people and, as a result, use them proactively. Yet, we rarely use this technique in our writings. No wonder most people find business books boring! By using beautiful stories from the art world, this book enlivens its subject matter and makes its messages memorable. Long after they have forgotten the main business message of a chapter, the reader will remember the stories described in that chapter.

Other books have used history, religion and biology to draw lessons for business managers. This book is one of the few to use the arts world for inspiration. It fills an important void and in the process makes a significant contribution.

Preface

There are hundreds of business books espousing "new" insights into key concepts in management. But most of these texts draw on well-known case studies and insights from the corporate world, often dressing existing frameworks in new management "buzz" words – but offering few new revelations. Very few discuss Picasso and Madonna as case studies for corporate success.

In this book we discuss successful strategies for driving innovation and creativity in the business world, but we do not turn to the analysis of well-known corporations such as Microsoft, IBM or Nokia. Instead, we examine the experiences of creative artists – from 16th Century painters such as Tizian and Tintoretto, to 19th and early 20th Century creative geniuses like van Gogh, Gauguin and Picasso, and contemporary artists such as Damien Hirst, Jeff Koons and Madonna. We suggest that the success stories of these artists have relevant lessons for contemporary managers – and the various chapters provide refreshing and entertaining case studies.

The business lessons from the world of creative arts have been under-researched to date due to the strong focus of faculty at most graduate management schools upon more traditionally defined private firms and publicly listed corporations. In addition, most academic research conducted in business schools focuses on the post-war period, with very few contemporary business academics delving back in time for historically relevant insights. The book is positioned in the fields of strategic management and marketing management. It aims to fill a vacuum in the business literature with regard to the insights and lessons for the world of business from the creative arts in the areas of innovation and creativity management. The book has been written for a global audience, and draws on case studies and examples from around the world. Many of the case studies we mention are recognized across borders, and the lessons communicated in the text are equally relevant for business managers in both developed and emerging markets.

The relevance of the book for both general and functional managers is demonstrated by the opening chapter on Madonna. The chapter suggests that continuous renewal of the organization is not just about crafting a detailed plan to be implemented without adaptation or evolution, but about establishing an overall direction that incorporates five key elements – vision, customer and industry insight, leveraging competences and weaknesses, consistent implementation, and a drive towards continuous renewal. This lesson is equally relevant for Chief Executive Officers (CEOs), Chief Marketing Officers (CMOs) or graduate students of management – and especially relevant at a time of economic crisis.

In Chapter 2, we turn to the topic of strategic innovation by examining the career of the 16th Century artist Tintoretto. We discuss how Tintoretto challenged the established art "industry" in his home city of Venice, which at the time was one of the world's great centres of art. We show how Tintoretto was able to create new market space in a "mature" industry dominated by the grand art master Titian. This chapter demonstrates that strategic innovation is not a new concept, but has been a lever for new value creation in different historical periods. Innovation is a key area for concern for modern businesses, and we provide lessons for how any contemporary business can leverage Tintoretto's approach for growth and profit.

Chapter 3 continues the theme of strategic innovation, but shifts from 16th Century Venice to the 21st Century contemporary art market. The chapter explores the controversial artist Damien Hirst, providing an overview of Hirst's career as an artist and the approach that has brought him wealth and success. Linking Hirst's success to that of Tintoretto some four centuries earlier, we demonstrate how modern day organizations can shake up an established industry structure and its key players merely by framing and answering the fundamental strategic questions "Who is the customer?", "What do I offer this customer?", and "How do I create value for the customer?" differently. After reflecting upon Hirst's career we turn to a discussion of companies that have strategically innovated in their own sectors.

In Chapter 4 we turn to the question of creativity, and how organization's can boost the creative potential of their people. Creativity is a widely used term in the context of strategy, innovation, organizational development and leadership. When managers realize that strategic questions, leadership issues and complex organizational situations are not manageable in a routine manner, the quest for creative solutions begins. The more unusual a situation, meaning that managers cannot draw upon experience or established routines, the more it calls for a creative solution. In that sense, creativity is seen almost as a prerequisite to manage change and renewal. Creativity is, therefore, a key skill for leaders and organizations, not only in order to adapt to change, but also to proactively shape industries and markets. "Think outside the box" is the slogan of countless creativity experts who rightly connect creative thinking to corporate innovation. But we advocate, instead, that managers think outside the canvas. A review of the thinking of the German artist, Joseph Beuys, shows how managers can unleash bold new ideas.

In Chapter 5 we return to the world of fine art to explore the 21st Century phenomenon of globalization, and how managers can draw upon the experience of artists to succeed in an increasingly global economy. The emergence of globalization in its current form has been seen as both a threat and an opportunity for firms, and has spurred an increasing interest in managing the global paradigm. We suggest that today's managers can learn much by stepping back and examining the manner in which artists adapted to the modern globalization of the arts from the mid-19th Century on. We present three different ways in which artists dealt with the modern globalization of the arts in the mid-19th Century: adoption, integration and fusion. *Adoption* was the way in which artists learned from foreign cultures by copying artistic techniques, concepts or approaches. Here Vincent Van Gogh's (1853–1890) experimentation with Japanese woodcuts is a good example. *Integration* was the approach adopted by artists such as Paul Gauguin who combined his experience of the world of Tahiti, with its light and colours, and a classical European understanding of composition. Finally we look at Picasso and realize that he created a completely new artistic approach out of different European and African influences through the act of *Fusion*.

In Chapter 6 we turn to the topic of leadership. How can managers affect the thoughts, feelings and behaviours of a significant number of individuals in a way that strategies are flawlessly and passionately executed across an organization? In this chapter we will take a close look at Jeff Koons, another successful and highly controversial contemporary artist, and explore the way in which he has projected himself as a credible leader in the world of contemporary art not at least through his way of telling a cohesive and convincing story through his artwork. Koons' work receives worldwide recognition and is shown in every major museum of modern art, like the three big New York museums The Museum of Modern Art, the Whitney and the Guggenheim. We suggest that Koons' use of storytelling, and the manner in which he has come to embody the themes and concepts that he seeks to communicate through his artworks, present powerful lessons for managers as to how they can manage their own leadership projection. By looking at Koons, managers can better understand not only how to establish credibility and drive buy-in, but also how to project themselves as leaders in their respective fields of business endeavour.

Chapter 7 looks at the video and performance artist Nam June Paik, who was able to over and over again juxtapose fields like art and music, east and west, technology and sexuality by embracing complexity, orchestrating creativity and emotionalizing his ideas. We feel that dealing with seemingly opposing ideas is a very typical dilemma not only for artists but also business men and women. Life seems to be an endless stream of trade-offs, either ors, decisions for cost or differentiation, lefts or rights. Therefore we believe that looking at an artist like Nam Jun Paik is worthwhile to deepen our understanding of how this might work. Born in Korea, having a US citizenship, being educated as musician, producing artwork, Paik incorporates the idea of innovation through juxtaposition. In this chapter we are closing in on Paik in order to better understand the potential of juxtaposition, of holding opposable positions in mind in order to envision and to create new solutions.

The last chapter is an interview with Gerrit Gohlke, executive director at artnet. artnet provides services to fine art professionals, like a price database, to bring price transparency to the art market, an online gallery network, building and hosting websites for art dealers and galleries on its platform, and an online art trade magazine. As a longstanding art market observer, Gerrit gives insights into the history and business model of artnet and more important on new trends in the art market, what artists can learn from managers and what managers can learn from artists and gallery owners and other stakeholders in the art industry.

Given its emphasis on the management of innovation and creativity, the book is written for general managers and graduate management students. It is appropriate for MBA courses in strategy, innovation management and marketing, and many of the case studies included in the text have already been used by the authors to teach graduate management students and executive education participants. But the various chapters also provide specific insights for functional managers, such as those working in new product development, innovation management, marketing and communications. At a time of global economic instability, fresh and innovative insights are needed for business; this book provides those insights.

About the Authors

Jamie Anderson is jointly Professor in Strategy and Innovation Management at Antwerp Management School, and the Lorange Institute Switzerland. He holds visiting positions at London Business School and the Indian School of Business. Jamie's research interests focus on strategy, innovation and corporate transformation, and his articles have appeared in publications such as *California Management Review*, *MIT Sloan Management Review*, *European Journal of Innovation Management*, the *Financial Times* and *Wall Street Journal*. He has presented as a business commentator on BBC World, CNN and CNBC. Jamie has developed executive education programs focused on strategy and Innovation for a range of Fortune 500 companies such as Deutsche Bank, Ericsson, Hewlett Packard, McDonalds, Nokia and Vodafone.

Jörg Reckhenrich is artist and founder of Art-Thinking Consulting, and Professor of Innovation and Creativity at the Lorange Institute, Switzerland. He is also visiting lecturer at London Business School and ESMT Berlin. He was recently named as one of the 'Top 25 Management Thinkers for 2009' by the management journal *Business Strategy Review*. He has developed, with his background as artist, an approach for executive learning that brings the creative principles of fine arts into the corporate field and has published widely on this approach, in journals like *Business Strategy Review, Rotman Magazine and the Economic Times of India.* Jörg has worked with various international companies, including Bombardier, Deutsche Bank, Mercedes Benz, Deutsche Bahn and British Petroleum. He has developed a proprietary approach for evaluating the creativity of top-level management in large corporations that has been adopted by a major international executive search firm.

Martin Kupp is a program director and member of the faculty at the European School of Management and Technology (ESMT), Berlin. His research interests focus on strategic innovation, corporate creativity and competitive strategy. Martin has widely published in journals like *California Management Review, MIT Sloan Management Review, Business Strategy Review, Wall Street Journal, Rotman Magazine and the Economic Times of India.* Martin has designed and taught on executive education programs for many multinational corporations like Allianz, Coca-Cola, MAN, Metro, Rosatom, Siemens, and ThyssenKrupp. He is an award winning case author, and conducts seminars on the writing and teaching of case studies at academic institutions around the world.

CHAPTER 1

Madonna
Strategy on the Dance Floor

The year 2009 saw Madonna Louise Veronica Ciccone Ritchie celebrate her 51st birthday and surpass cumulative album sales of 200 million to become the top selling female rock artist of the 20th Century. Just two years earlier Guinness World Records had listed her as the world's most successful female recording artist of all time, and she was subsequently inducted into the Rock and Roll Hall of Fame. In 2008 she released her 11th studio album titled *Hard Candy* which became another of her albums to debut at number one on the Billboard albums chart, embarked on yet another top-selling world tour and collaborated on a number of new tracks with Justin Timberlake and Timbaland, two of the world's hottest young music stars. Her marriage to film director husband Guy Ritchie came to an end, and she embarked on a controversial second adoption of a child from Africa; but the publicity surrounding these events seemed to do little to dent her professional achievements. So how has Madonna been able to maintain her incredible success? The answer to this question lies in five key ingredients of successful strategy that are equally relevant to companies and individual managers. These five dimensions have provided the foundation underpinning Madonna's stardom, and if diligently pursued can provide the ingredients for sustained company and career success. Indeed, without these elements in place an organization will not have the foundations upon which to drive innovation and creativity.

Dimension 1 – Vision

One of the most important drivers of Madonna's success has been her desire to achieve stardom – her strategic *vision*. Madonna has demonstrated a clear commitment to her super-stardom goal that has been pursued with single mindedness throughout her career.

Madonna is the third of eight children and her mother died at the age of 30, of breast cancer in 1963, when Madonna was only five. The singer has frequently discussed the enormous impact her mother's death had on her life and career, and being the eldest daughter of a large Catholic family meant that a greater share of household and emotional responsibilities fell on Madonna's young shoulders. Her aspiration to be a performer started at High School, where she was a straight-A student and excelled at sport, dance and drama. She continued her interest in dance during brief periods at colleges in Michigan and North Carolina, and in 1977 went to New York, studying with noted choreographer Alvin Ailey and taking modelling jobs. Two years later, Madonna moved to France to join a show featuring disco singer Patrick Hernandez. There she met musician Dan Gilroy and, back in New York, the pair formed club band The

Breakfast Club. Madonna played drums and sang with the band before setting up pop group Emmy in 1980 with Detroit-born drummer and former boyfriend, Steve Bray. Together, Madonna and Bray created club tracks which led to a recording deal with Sire Records. With leading New York disc jockey Mark Kamins producing, she recorded "Everybody", a US club hit in 1982.

Between 1983 and 2009, more than ten studio albums, multiple world tours, and a dozen or so movie roles had established Madonna with an image and persona beyond any single field of entertainment: she was musician, actor, author and talent scout. In delivering upon her vision she has also made a great deal of money: she is easily the world's top earning female entertainer. Madonna's vision to become a star has been clearly apparent, and her spectrum of personal and professional activities – stage performances, television appearances, albums, music videos, Hollywood films, books and links to charity – all evidence a remarkable dedication to a single goal: the objective of becoming the world's foremost female performer.

Vision is equally important for organizations that wish to achieve long-term success. The Virgin Group Ltd is an entity consisting of many separately run companies united by the Virgin brand of British celebrity business tycoon Sir Richard Branson. The Virgin Group's core businesses are travel, entertainment and lifestyle, and Virgin is one of the UK's best known consumer brands, associated with excellent service and having the consumers' interests at heart. In the words of Richard Branson: "I look for opportunities where we can offer something better, fresher and more valuable . . . I think one of the reasons for our success is the core values which Virgin aspires to. This includes those that the general public thinks we should aspire to, like providing quality service. However, we also promise value for money, and we try to do things in an innovative way, in areas where consumers are often ripped-off, or not getting the most for their money. I believe we should do what we do with a sense of fun and without taking ourselves too seriously, too! If Virgin stands for anything, it should be for not being afraid to try out new ideas in new areas." This vision to win in markets through the delivery of service excellence, value for money and innovation has remained consistent for more than three decades.

A good example of how the Virgin Group's philosophy translates into a vision to succeed in a specific market place has been seen in the firm's success in the UK mobile communications sector. After launching its operations as a mobile virtual network operator (MVNO) in November 1999, Virgin Mobile (VM) proved to be one of the remarkable success stories of the UK mobile phone industry. With a steadfast vision to become the customer champion in the 18–35 year-old prepay segment, VM was able to achieve a number of significant milestones right from its inception. With a steadfast focus on its target customer group, by June 2001 it had captured more than one million customers, making it the fastest (among the major UK mobile communications providers) to have achieved that milestone. Within five years of launch the company had an active customer base of over four million and its customers were found to be among the most satisfied in the pre-pay sector, according to surveys conducted by J.D. Power and Associates. VM had also been included in "The Sunday Times 100 Best Companies to Work For" and was part of the FTSE4Good. The company was recognized as the most admired brand in the UK with a distinct customer proposition and market positioning.

VM UK believed its strong growth had been driven by clear vision, its brand and differentiated approach to the market. The brand was consumer rather than technology-oriented, and this strategic message remained consistent from inception in 1999. While other mobile network operators in the UK had broad visions to be all things to all customers, Virgin's vision and strategic focus allowed it to build an organizational culture, structures and processes that were in complete alignment with its core value proposition and target market.

Dimension 2 – Understanding Customers and Industry

It is clear that Madonna's success has been underpinned through her deep and insightful appreciation of customers and understanding of the music industry. Madonna's performance at the First Annual MTV Video Music Awards in 1984 at the age of 26 is considered to be the first stroke of genius in a career that would see many more. She took the stage to sing "Like A Virgin" wearing a combination bustier and wedding gown. During the performance, she rolled around on the floor, revealing lacy stockings and garters, and made a number of sexually suggestive moves. The performance was shocking to a mid-1980s audience, but only served to increase her popularity with her main target group, teenage fans. Showing her ability to tap into youth sub-culture, Madonna's bleached blonde hair with brown roots, sexy lace gloves, lingerie on the outside and "Boy Toy" belt buckle defined teen-pop fashion of the era.

Beyond an ability to understand the needs and tastes of current customers, Madonna has also shown an ability to tap into evolving trends. While focus groups have been used to help sell everything from washing powder to political parties, Madonna has been one of the world's first artists to bring this approach to the music industry. Showing her ability to interpret the needs of the market, in mid-2005 Madonna partnered with DJ and producer Stuart Price, age 28, to test songs in clubs from Liverpool to Ibiza. The tunes, with Madonna's distinctive vocals removed, were played and the reactions of the crowds were filmed and used to determine the final track listing of *Confessions on a Dance Floor*. According to Price: "Whenever I was DJ-ing I'd take dub or instrumental versions out with me and test them at the club that night". He said, "I had my camera with me and the next day I'd tell Madonna, 'This is what a thousand people in Liverpool look like dancing to our song.'" He added, "You can work on a song for 12 hours but I guarantee you'll know within just 10 seconds of putting it on at a club whether it works or not." Within the first week of release, the lead track from *Confessions on a Dance Floor* "Hung Up" became the number one download on iTunes stores around the world, and went on to top the charts in an unprecedented 45 countries. Madonna's "Confessions Tour" began in May 2006, had a global audience of 1.2 million people and reported gross sales of $260.1 million – the highest earning pop tour of all time.

Madonna has also shown expertise in understanding and shaping the music industry. She has the ability to shape her image in the media, and has been recognized as a skilled self-publicist – a critical ingredient for success in an industry that sees new competitors entering on an almost daily basis. Understanding that the music industry is heavily influenced by very few big players like MTV and the big record labels she teamed up with MTV very early in her career. Her first album sold only moderately at first, but thanks to heavy rotation on MTV, Madonna gained nationwide exposure and the album peaked at number eight on the Billboard chart, and went platinum five times. It ultimately sold close to ten million copies worldwide. MTV aggressively marketed Madonna's image as a playful and sexy combination of punk and pop culture, and she soon became closely allied with the network.

In 1987 Madonna embarked on the "Who's That Girl World Tour" and the tour marked her first run-in with the Vatican when the Pope urged fans not to attend her performances in Italy. The fans were not affected, however, and the tour went on as scheduled. Her use of sex as a marketing tool brought her fame and notoriety in the early 1990s, when she became one of the world's first mass-market performers to manipulate the juxtaposition of sexual and religious themes. The music video for her chart-topping song "Like a Prayer" featured many Catholic symbols, and was denounced by the Vatican for its "blasphemous" mixture of sexual themes and Catholic symbolism. Madonna had signed a deal with Pepsi according to which the song "Like a Prayer" would be debuted as a Pepsi commercial. When Madonna's own music video version of the song debuted on MTV, Pepsi pulled theirs off the air. But Madonna got to keep her $5 million dollar endorsement fee without fulfilling her contractual obligations. In 2003 Madonna again stirred controversy at MTV when she kissed her "brides", Britney Spears and Christina Aguilera, on stage during the MTV Video Music Awards. The use of religious symbols such as the crucifix in her 2006 "Confessions on a Dance Floor Tour" caused the Russian Orthodox Church and the Federation of Jewish Communities of Russia to urge people to boycott her concert. The Vatican as well as bishops from Germany also protested. Madonna responded that, "My performance is neither anti-Christian, sacrilegious or blasphemous. Rather, it is my plea to the audience to encourage mankind to help one another and to see the world as a unified whole."

But despite these events, Madonna has shown a deep understanding of the politics of the music industry, and has proven to be skilled at walking the line between the shocking and sacrificing her career. She has worked particularly hard to maintain positive and mutually beneficial relations with major music companies such as MTV, and has avoided the fate of artists such as Sinead O'Connor who's political activism saw her shunned from the major distribution channels needed to link to fans.

In an increasingly competitive and global world, customer and industry understanding is also a necessity for companies and managers. Poor attention to industry dynamics and evolving customer needs can result in companies being side-stepped by their rivals. A good example of this has been the German retail banking sector where an aging population, increasingly sophisticated consumers, technological changes and the entry of new competitors has witnessed the profitability of German retail banks decline considerably over the past decade. The vast majority of German banks have been very slow to respond to these changes, while new competitors have stepped forward to implement new business models more in tune with the emerging financial services requirements.

Ranking only behind the US and Japan, the German economy is the world's third largest. Post-war economic growth has provided German citizens with one of the world's highest standards of living. But Germany's formerly affluent and technologically powerful economy turned in a relatively weak performance throughout much of the 1990s, and the economic downturn of 2008–2009 may well herald the prospect of low growth for the foreseeable future.

Germany's total estimated population is 82 million, and modest population growth estimates put the levels at 85 million by 2015. There are now 2.6 working age Germans for every person aged 60 or older. Demographic trends similar to those being experienced in other developing countries project that figure dropping to 1.4 by 2030. In just a few years, there will be more people aged 65 and over than people aged 15 years or under. The number of people over 80 will increase to around three times as many by 2050, while the number of people over 100 will increase to around six times as many by 2050. There are currently two workers per retiree, but if current demographic trends continue by 2050 there will be less than one worker per retiree.

Structural rigidities – like a high rate of social contributions to wages – and the impact on industry of the economic crisis of 2008–2009 have made unemployment a long-term, not just a cyclical, problem, while Germany's aging population has pushed social security outlays to exceed contributions from workers. A recent study by the Centre for European Reform reported that if Germany were to rely on immigrants to keep its ratio of workers to pensioners constant, its population would consist of 80 percent foreigners by 2050. There is an almost unanimous view in both government and industry that Germany faces a massive pensions shortfall within a generation. Not surprisingly, fewer than 50 percent of people in Germany between the ages of 18 and 35 think that their finances will be "good" or "very good" in retirement.

The comparison with the pension systems in other industrial nations underlines the structural deficits of the German system. In Germany 85 percent of pensions are currently financed by state funds. Only some 5 percent come from company pensions schemes, while the remaining 10 percent are made up of private policies. In the US, for example, state-funded pensions and private pension plans each make up around 40–45 percent of total pensions, while 13 percent of pensions are company policies. In the Netherlands the state-funded proportion is only some 50 percent, while company policies account for 40 percent. The remaining 10 percent then comes from private policies.

Despite deep structural problems related to its aging population and pension needs, one of Germany's strengths is its gross domestic savings rate, which has remained around the 10th highest in the world over the past few decades. The total value of inherited assets in Germany in the 1990s was €1.3 trillion. Inherited assets of €2.3 trillion are expected for the period between 2010 and 2020. Historically, Germans have saved primarily via low interest *Sparbuch* savings accounts, and until the 1990s, more than half of private savings were regularly deposited with banks. Analysts suggest that the increase in private assets naturally will lead to a greater demand for investment opportunities. Clients, they suggest, will demand individual products that allow them to meet their personal investment aims and return expectations.

Despite the potentially significant opportunities to support Germans with their financial planning needs, German banks have languished near the bottom of the performance league when compared to their peers in many other developed countries such as the US and the UK. The return on assets for the main UK banks was over four times higher than for the big German private sector banks over the period 2000–2005; and cost income ratios were more than 30 percent lower. In consequence the market capitalization of German banks has traditionally been very low. The German commercial banks have typically blamed labour laws, the pricing policies of state funded competitors and the low customer propensity to borrow for their failure to restructure. But instead of pointing to the customer or the competitor – management should have instead focused on delivering operational efficiency and innovation to provide new products and services.

While most of the established retail banks in Germany have been slow to respond to changes in the industry environment, more nimble competitors such as financial advisory firm MLP have stepped forward to take advantage of changing customer needs. In 2008 the MLP Group was one of the largest and most profitable financial advisory firms in the German retail financial services industry, but outside of its home country almost nobody knew its name. MLP's 262 branches and 2,613 consultants made it one of Europe's largest independent financial services firms. Its after-tax return on equity had averaged 21 percent since 1998, more than ten times that of some of its competitors in the industry. In some years ROE had exceeded 40 percent, and MLP had been voted German Company of the Year five times by *Manager Magazine.*

As an independent broker, it is MLP's vision to provide discerning clients with integrated financial services and to be the best partner for them at every stage of their lives for pension, asset management and risk management. MLP's focus is on distinct professional groups, such as doctors and lawyers, economists and scientists, IT-specialists, engineers and academics, who the company believes have high future earning potential and attractive risk profiles. In principle, its main clients are university educated men and women who the firm has served since their graduation.

With its unique business model that brings together a federation of highly entrepreneurial financial consultants, MLP has built a reputation for clients with sophisticated requirements on pension provision, asset management and risk management. By the beginning of 2008 MLP counted more than 721,000 clients and firmly believed that Germany's aging population and emerging pension crisis places it in a strong position for future success. In the words of Dr Uwe Schroeder-Wildberg, MLP CEO;

> *Based upon a foundation of a tried and tested business model our company has worked to become an independent financial service provider in an excellent market position, which will enable us to benefit from long-term market developments. And more tail wind will also come from demographic and political developments.*

The German retail financial services industry has changed dramatically since the late 1990s. Deregulation, globalization and pension reform, among other factors, have contributed to massive turbulence in a once conservative and stable environment. The slowness of most German retail banks to adapt to these challenges has seen their profitability steadily decline, while firms such as MLP have stepped forward to win customers and profits. Just like Madonna, MLP has understood the significance of shifts in the industry landscape.

Dimension 3 – Leveraging Competences and Addressing Weaknesses

Another important element in Madonna's success has been the ability to acknowledge her own competencies and weaknesses. Looking at her impressive career it becomes obvious that one of Madonna's most outstanding competencies is her ability to bring people with various talents together with herself as the hub. Through the use of her extensive network of support personnel, including musicians, technologists, producers, dancers and designers she is able to address her weaknesses and even compensate for them.

Very early on in her career Madonna realized that her dancing abilities and her voice were not strong enough on their own. She started to team up. One of her first and probably most important and successful alliances started in 1982. She flew to Los Angeles to convince Michael Jackson's manager, Freddie De Mann, to help her launch her music career. De Mann did just that, and eventually dropped Jackson altogether. In 1983 her self-titled first album, *Madonna*, was released, and its hit single, "Holiday" was Madonna's first top 20 hit single in several countries. Other hits on *Madonna* included "Borderline" and "Lucky Star". The album was produced with contributions from John "Jellybean" Benitez, with whom Madonna had also had a brief romance.

Madonna's debut as an actor followed her marriage to Hollywood actor Sean Penn, and a brief relationship with Warren Beatty. Her book *Sex* was released as an accompaniment to her studio album *Erotica* as the first output of a recently signed partnership with Time Warner. Undertaken with the support of famous friends from the music, film and fashion industries, Time Warner commented that *Sex* was very complex to produce, requiring partnerships with many different printing and publishing companies. The photographs in the book were taken by some of the world's best known fashion photographers – Steven Meisel, Fabian Baron, Stephen Callaghan and Darren Lew. *Sex* stirred significant controversy for its sexually explicit content but went on to sell 1,500,000 copies at a cover price of $50 within three days of release. This made *Sex* the fastest selling coffee table book of all time, and an additional million copies each were printed in French, Japanese and Italian. Featured in the book were model Naomi Campbell, actress Isabella Rossellini, rap performers Vanilla Ice and Big Daddy Kane, gay porn actor Udo Kier, and the European socialite Tatiana von Furstenberg. The day after the release of the book cable television company MTV screened a documentary called *The Day In Madonna* featuring Madonna's *Sex* and her new album *Erotica*.

In December 2000 at the age of 42, Madonna married film director Guy Ritchie. In June 2001, she appeared in *Star*, a short commercial film directed for BMW by Ritchie, and then began working on *Swept Away*. Her partnership with UK DJ Stuart Price towards the *Confessions on a Dance Floor* album has been mentioned above, and in 2007 she partnered with world-renowned artists Justin Timberlake and Timbaland towards the creation of her *Hard Candy* album, moving from the disco sounds of *Confessions on a Dance Floor* to the rhythm of R&B. The single "4 Minutes" that she produced with Timberlake and Timbaland resulted in Madonna's 37th Billboard Top 100 top ten hit, thus surpassing Elvis Presley as the artist with the most top ten hits.

Capability and skills gaps can also be a critical barrier to the success of firms, so managers need to understand areas of strength and weakness and how to develop capabilities through development activities, partnerships, networks or alliances. When VM sought to enter the UK mobile phone sector it recognized that it was lacking a very critical resource – a mobile network. The company saw the cost of a license to enter the mobile sector as an independent operator as prohibitively expensive, and instead sought to partner with one of the existing players. VM UK was floated as a joint venture between Virgin and T-Mobile in 1999, and Virgin operated as an MVNO to be able to provide cellular services without owning wireless spectrum access rights. To customers, Virgin looked like any other cellular operator, giving the impression of a full-fledged mobile operator. But the company did not own or operate base station infrastructure. For T-Mobile, the main benefit of the partnership with Virgin was to tap into consumers with whom it had a low brand affinity, therefore having a low risk of self cannibalization, and to maximize utilization of its network capacity thereby achieving greater economies of scale.

Being an MVNO, Virgin needed less capital. The company did not have to invest in network hardware. Because of its partnership with T-Mobile, it already had access on long-term contractual terms to billions of pounds' worth of state-of-the-art mobile network assets. The company enjoyed the scale benefits of the network operators, without the associated investment and technology risk. Although other incumbent operators could realize the benefits of scale once their large fixed cost base was covered, VM had a very low fixed cost base compared to traditional mobile network operators – for example, Virgin's capital expenditure (CAPEX) as a percentage of earnings averaged around 2 percent compared to more than 20 percent for some industry incumbents. Even a teenage subscriber spending just a few pounds each month could contribute value to Virgin. In the words of Tom Alexander, former CEO of VM UK:

> There's no great mystery to Virgin Mobile's approach. We are a marketing and service business: we focus on customers, not engineering; we focus on the brand experience, not technology. We give our customers what they want – not what's easiest for us to provide. And what our customers want is exactly what we stand for: value for money, outstanding service, great products and a sense of fun . . . Because we're not a network operator, we're free to focus on people, not hardware. We focus on our own people, through our singular Virgin Mobile culture; and we focus on our customers, by providing them the best customer service in the business . . . Attention to the needs of our customers – in our role as the Consumer Champion – is at the heart of everything we do.

In addition to compensating for potential weaknesses, VM was also able to leverage its core strengths in service delivery and retail distribution to enter the UK mobile market. Effective and targeted distribution played a key role in the company's success, and in just five years, the company had built a distribution network of around 6,000 sales outlets, with another 50,000 outlets selling airtime. The company capitalized on the value of the Virgin brand by putting dedicated VM "stores within stores" inside 96 Virgin Megastores nationally, many staffed by dedicated, expert sales people. Each store stocked the entire range of products. In addition, there were a total of 104 VM stores throughout the UK in 2005 where only Virgin's services were sold.

VM stores were designed to offer customers a unique experience – as the perfect environment to showcase VM's products and services. Customers were made to feel relaxed and staff made a point of being friendly but not "salesy". VM's in-store "experts" were trained to be open, honest and knowledgeable, and to help bring VM to life. Customers could try before they bought a phone to see if the phone was right for them, and self-service interactive kiosks showed customers the range of VM products and services on offer. According to Tom Alexander: "We hand-pick our VM Stores staff. They're warm and friendly, they always give their best, they like talking to people . . . and we're proud of them!"

Virgin also used its expertise in distribution to build a network of distribution alliances. Virgin innovated by being the first mobile company to offer its products through such well-known high street stores as Woolworths, Comet, Argos, Sainsbury's, Tesco and Asda. The high street channel was particularly attractive for Virgin as these retailers typically charged lower commissions than traditional industry channels. Virgin's extensive use of retailers was an important difference between its distribution approach and the approach of the established mobile network operators. For example, Virgin's competitors Vodafone and O2 reported 40–50 percent of their sales were attributable to owned retail channels in 2005, while for VM this number was only 22 percent.

Just as Madonna has leveraged her strengths and overcome her weaknesses, VM succeeded in the UK mobile telecommunications sector by taking a similar approach. The company's strong foundation in customer service and retail distribution provided a perfect complement to the technology expertise brought by its network partner T-Mobile.

Dimension 4 – Consistent Implementation

Madonna has also been able to stay on top through an impressive ability to implement her strategy. Perhaps most impressive is the fact that Madonna is not the product of any music company – her success has been very much the outcome of her hard work and ability to get the job done. Despite the increasing dominance of the global media sector by multinational firms such as Warner Brothers, Sony, Bertelsmann and Vivendi Universal, Madonna has maintained her independence while expanding her influence.

Despite the radio success of "Justify My Love" in 1990, the sexual content of both the song's lyrics and video saw the song embargoed by network executives at MTV. In response, Madonna's record company decided to sell the video as the world's first ever "video single". The video sold over 400,000 copies, and the CD single went on to sell over one million.

Most of Madonna's entertainment interests have been owned and operated by her own companies. In 1992, Madonna founded entertainment company Maverick as a joint venture with Time Warner. Maverick consisted of a record company (Maverick Records), a film production company (*Maverick Films*) and also music publishing, television, merchandising and book-publishing divisions. The seven-year multimedia contract was reportedly worth $60 million and gave Madonna almost complete artistic control over her music – including her own record label. Included in the package were deals for cable-TV specials, books and any film projects she wished to develop, plus a share of the profits generated by other Maverick artists. By the mid-1990s, Madonna had become an active chief executive of the Maverick label. Maverick's roster included Me'Shell NdegeOcello – who performed on *Bedtime Stories* – heavy grunge rockers Candlebox, and Bad Brains.

Madonna announced her departure from Warner Bros. Records in 2007 and a new $120 million, ten-year contract with events management company Live Nation. Mainly a concert promoter, Live Nation "signs" artists as a "record label", but predominantly takes the role of a promoter rather than "owner of music". Annually Live Nation promotes or produces over 22,000 events, including music concerts, theatrical shows and other events, with total attendance exceeding 50 million. As part of the Live Nation partnership, Madonna became the founding recording artist for a new music division, Live Nation Artists. In 2008–2009 Madonna embarked on the "Sticky and Sweet Tour" to promote her *Hard Candy* album, which was her first major venture with Live Nation. It became the highest-grossing tour ever by a solo artist with gross earnings of $280 million, surpassing the record previously held by her "Confessions on a Dance Floor Tour".

Implementation is also key for organizations and the people within them – strategy is the easy part, but as any wise manager knows the devil is in the detail of getting the job done. Many companies spend months or years on elaborate strategies while failing to develop the structures, processes and mindset to implement them. The electronics and technology giant Philips took decades to re-invent its business. A string of CEOs at the Netherlands-based company did not lack strategic intent, but implementation across the organization's notoriously political operating companies proved an arduous task.

Effective implementation has been key to the drive by Germany's MLP to take advantage of shifts in the country's market for retail financial services. At year end 2008, MLP employed 1,800 employees in addition to its 2,613 consultants. The headquarters operation provides key areas of functional support such as human resources (including recruitment and training), quality management, accounting, sales support and marketing. Another important headquarters' responsibility is asset collection and management.

Unlike the branches of its banking rivals, MLP branch offices are rarely located on the ground floor of busy high streets. The vast majority of new client business for MLP comes via referrals, and appointments with consultants are almost always scheduled. MLP does not rely on "drop-in" business, and indeed such business is not encouraged as the company has a highly focused customer segmentation and does not seek to serve any "walk-in" customer.

Therefore, its branches tend to be found in convenient although not high-profile down-town locations. MLP also locates its branches on university campuses. This strategic placement of branches has an added advantage for MLP – rental costs per square metre are typically much less for its office locations than for those of its main competitors.

Branch facilities are simple but adequate. There is a shared waiting area for clients, and each consultant has his or her own small office. MLP consultants rent their computer from headquarters, and pay for all consumables used in the branch such as stationary, marketing materials and coffee for clients. Consultants' offices are furnished according to individual tastes, but it is rare to see advertising posters or brochures for investment products. According to one MLP client: "It is very different to walking into the formality of a big bank. My consultant's office is more like a personal space than a place to do business. He has some art prints on the wall, and pictures of his children on his desk. It doesn't feel like my money is being spent to pay the rent."

The branch manager is typically an experienced consultant with more than five years experience, and is responsible for the performance of the branch. The manager typically has only 50–80 active customers, and receives a share of the commission's of his or her branch consultants. The organization also appoints regional managers to coordinate clusters of branch offices. Each branch office has one or two administrative assistants to support the resident consultants and branch manager.

The sales support organization is divided by product group and screens the market to select appropriate investments for the MLP product portfolio. It has a research area that monitors the performance of funds and other products, and sets commission rates and product prices. In the area of marketing, the sales support organization produces marketing materials and product information that can be purchased by individual consultants, and monitors consultant compliance to corporate brand guidelines.

MLP has invested €25 million annually in IT over the past decade, with around one-quarter of its headquarters employees being engaged in IT-related tasks. As the first priority these employees organize data so that it is possible to identify, at any time, information coming from or going to a particular customer. MLP has developed its own software solutions in the areas of data organization, product advice, creation of new products and assembly of savings plans from different components.

In other areas, where there is no need for specialized know-how, standard software tends to be installed. In order to focus on content rather than on the technical aspects of information management, MLP outsources IT services to Hewlett Packard. Rather than asking an external partner to take over its entire IT infrastructure, MLP has handed over responsibility for the operation of its network and computer centre. It retains direct responsibility for strategic issues, such as the effective use of IT to communicate with customers, or the choice of partner to work with on different tasks.

MLP has developed five core SAP-based IT applications: logging consulting services (Clickstream Live), maintaining existing policies and new business (Policies), central reporting for all operational systems (Partner Inventory Live), Internet-based applicant placement (Career Base) and employee planning for graduate support (Potential Live). Potential Live is a particularly important application that enables MLP to determine the number of graduates (approximately 120,000 per year) in the occupational categories which MLP targets. This information enables MLP to strategically plan personnel capacities well in advance, to provide the best possible service to graduates.

MLP sets a limit of maximum 200 active clients per advisor because it believes the fewer clients its consultants have to consult the better they are able to consult each individual. Consultants typically meet their clients once or twice a year. MLP has three key values underpinning its consultancy business:

1. **Per consultant MLP concentrates on a maximum of 200 active clients**, simply because the fewer clients consultants have, the more time and energy they will have to invest in each individual client.

2. **Consultants with same or similar academic backgrounds and degrees as clients are made available to MLP's academic clients.** This means consultants know where their clients are headed and find themselves in the best position to help them achieve their objectives.

3. **Maximizing value added.** Consultants' valuable advisory time is held free through the support offered by MLP's Back Office, which does research and keeps its consultants informed about the latest developments on the financial markets.

MLP consultants work hard to build up their own client base. The organization does little consumer marketing in the media, with most of its new business coming from direct referrals and promotional activities undertaken by advisors themselves. Consultants are required to purchase all of their own marketing materials, and these are provided by the central sales support organization.

University campuses provide a key source of new clients and MLP advisors attend graduation celebrations to meet prospective clients, running special activities and events to promote the organization. On campus promotional activities often involve several branches and dozens of consultants, and are carefully coordinated in close cooperation between branch managers.

Advisors endeavour to contact new graduates within a month of leaving university to set up an initial appointment to discuss their financial future. A "client" does not usually become profitable until five years after commencing employment, although MLP offers a free current account and other limited services to its target customers during this "transition" phase from student to young career professional.

MLP looks to recruit college-graduates and especially "academics" and professionals with work experience. The company also recruits from the financial services industry, although consultants coming from banking and insurance represent a small share of total employees. A university degree is advantageous, but is not essential – what MLP really seeks is intelligence, entrepreneurship and strong social skills. Entrepreneurship is a particularly important attribute given the fact that MLP consultants do not receive a salary beyond the initial training period – remuneration is completely performance based.

In the two-year training course to become an MLP Financial Consultant, candidates go through more than 700 teaching units. In the years that follow, MLP consultants continue to expand their knowledge in all facets of financial services through a further central training programme. Consultants undertake 72 days of training at MLP's Corporate University in the first year of employment, and subsequently 27 days per year at the headquarters and 60 days per year in the branch office. MLP Corporate University has a total training capacity of 270,000 days per year. After two years advisors become "senior consultants" and are able to offer the full range of MLP products.

Just like MLP, Madonna has known the importance of planning and implementation all along – she has just not broadcast the fact. She once reportedly admitted: "Part of the reason I'm successful is because I'm a good businesswoman, but I don't think it necessary for people to know that."

Dimension 5 – Continuous Renewal

The fourth element to Madonna's success has been her ability to renew her popularity again and again. Within a year of the commercial flop of her *American Life* album she embarked on her "Re-Invention World Tour", during which she played 56 dates across the world. The tour became the world's highest-grossing tour of 2004, earning more than $100 million. Compare her abilities in re-invention to many "one-hit-wonders" in the music industry, or to performers such as the Rolling Stones who have enjoyed long periods of success, but whose fan-base has aged or remained largely unchanged.

The frequent re-invention of Madonna's style and sound has reflected an acute awareness of changing styles, social norms and attitudes in a fast clock-speed industry. From her punk-pop look of the early 1980s, her ever growing fan base has witnessed multiple reincarnations. These have included her glam-rock look of the late 1980s, a Marilyn Monroe retro look, her soft-core porn image of the early 1990s (which included a documentary film *In Bed with Madonna* and the release of her bestselling book *Sex*, which showed Madonna as the centrepiece of photographs depicting various sexual fantasies), her high-fashion look of the mid 1990s, a spiritual image that accompanied motherhood in the late 1990s and her disco look associated with the release of *Confessions on a Dance Floor*. Perhaps not surprisingly she is known as the "queen of re-invention" within industry circles.

Some say that in the corporate world you cannot teach old dogs new tricks. But companies that are "one-trick ponies" can expect market derailment unless they are able to renew and re-invent themselves. Witness the challenges faced by firms across history in industries such as chemical photography, printed encyclopaedias and department store retailing that have struggled to re-invent themselves in the face of industry disruption. Just a handful of firms, such as Finland's Nokia, have shown an uncanny ability to radically redefine their businesses to respond to evolving industry trends and customer tastes. Nokia started out as a manufacturer of paper in 1865, but has evolved its business through industries including rubber, electric cables, consumer electronics, personal computers, mobile phones and networking technologies. The company's most recent foray is into outsourced services, as it looks to manage the mobile networks of telecommunications companies in developed and developing markets.

Another firm that has managed to adapt to changing industry environment is VM of the UK. As mentioned above, VM had carved out a highly differentiated niche in the UK mobile market during the first five years of its existence. While its main rivals had attempted to serve a wide range of customer segments with broad product and service portfolios, Virgin had remained highly focused on its target customer segment. But by mid-2005 some analysts were questioning the sustainability of Virgin's strategy in the face of a number of new developments. The most tangible example of higher competition in the UK had been the launch of EasyMobile, a 50:50 JV between EasyGroup and TDC, a Danish network operator that had been challenged by low-cost MVNOs in its home market. VM's share price fell 15 percent within days of the EasyGroup announcement of its intention to launch a mobile offer.

Following EasyMobile's launch one of the UK's biggest mobile retailers Carphone Warehouse reduced tariffs on its own MVNO Fresh to make them mildly cheaper than those offered by EasyMobile. In addition to the new pricing pressure from EasyMobile's arrival and aggressive tariffs from Fresh, the UK market was being impacted by the aggression of new entrant Hutchison "3" that saw its market share grow rapidly. By mid 2005 "3" was adding over 60,000 new customers per week, and reported a customer base of 3.2 million. "3" believed that it would hit the four million customer mark by the end of the year. Tesco Mobile, a 50:50 joint venture by the Tesco supermarket chain and O2, was another new entrant that had shown significant customer momentum since launch in late 2004, with some 750,000 customers signed up in the first six months and a target of two million by the end of 2005.

The established operators had not sat still in the face of actions by companies such as "3" and Tesco. O2 had won significant prepay market share in 2004–2005 with new offers – adding 1.1 million new customers. France Telecom's Orange also launched a series of special promotions in 2004 based around "tailor-made" monthly programmes, while Vodafone had launched a concerted marketing campaign to target what it described as the "young, active, fun" segment via its Vodafone Live! Portal, new prepay packages and a marketing campaign with British footballer David Beckham. T-Mobile UK had been working to increase its store base, build brand and grow customer acquisition through a more aggressive approach to the market.

In the face of intensified competition, VM's percentage share of new customers slowed significantly in 2005, and its prices were being significantly undercut by the competition. Perhaps not surprising given this intense competition, Virgin stated in early 2005 that advertising and customer acquisition and retention costs would rise, and predicted decreased profit margins. In addition, termination rates (the money Virgin received for terminating a call from another network operator's customers to one of its own customers) were cut by 30 percent by the UK regulator in September 2004. This was forecast to result in gross margins for inbound calls declining by more than 10 percent.

The relatively stable competitive and regulatory situation that VM had experienced over the period 1999–2005 was changing rapidly, and management recognized that something had to be done should the company wish to maintain profitability and growth. Competitive advantage is a dynamic process, and Virgin's management were quickly coming to understand that changes in the competitive environment could undermine even seemingly unique market positions. But what should the company do to respond to the intense competition now enveloping the UK mobile telecoms sector?

In 2006 Richard Branson announced that he had sold a majority stake in VM to the cable network operator NTL for close to a billion pounds. The acquisition brought together NTL's technological expertise with Virgin's strengths in customer service. Indeed, NTL's management described the merger of the two organizations as more than just a new name and logo – it signalled a completely fresh start for NTL which had previously been known for its strong product offerings but poor customer focus. The new company would be built around Virgin's core values of value for money, brilliant customer service, good quality, innovation and fun. In 2007 the merged company was rebranded Virgin Media, and became the only multimedia company in the UK to be able to offer full quadruple-play services: mobile telephony, fixed telephony, broadband and pay television. This represented a strategic transformation, with Virgin and NTL departing from their respective industries of mobile telephony and cable TV to enter the newly emerging market space for converged telecommunication, Internet and media services. Just like Madonna, they had strategically re-invented themselves to stay ahead of the competition in a dynamic and rapidly changing business environment.

Conclusion

Few would argue that Madonna lacks the voice of Anastasia, the acting ability of Nicole Kidman or the song writing talent of Justin Timberlake. While she is undoubtedly in excellent physical condition, few would regard her as beautiful as Jennifer Lopez or Mariah Carey. Her various acting roles have rarely attracted anything but scathing criticism and her 2003 album *American Life* was panned by critics, who described it as an indication that she was "in need of a vacation" from the stress of her career. But despite apparent gaps in her capabilities and the occasional setback, she has been able to reincarnate her career time and time again.

As Madonna has demonstrated, strategy is not about crafting a detailed plan to be implemented without adaptation or evolution, but about establishing an overall direction that incorporates five key elements – vision, customer and industry insight, leveraging competences and weaknesses, consistent implementation, and a drive towards continuous innovation and renewal. These five elements are as equally important to companies such as Virgin, Nokia and MLP as they are to global pop-stars, and organizations that fail to take into account all of these dimensions risk being sidelined by more nimble and strategically oriented competitors.

In mid 2009 Madonna started working on *Celebrations* her third "greatest hits" album and was in the process of planning her next world tour in partnership with Live Nation. Her adoption of Mercy James, the second controversial adoption from Malawi in just two years, had been approved by the Supreme Court of Malawi and *Forbes Magazine* had just named her as the third most powerful celebrity of the year. After two and a half decades at the top of her profession there was little indication that Madonna's career was slowing down.

ELEMENTS OF MADONNA'S SUCCESS

1. **Vision.** Madonna has demonstrated a clear commitment to superstardom goal that was pursued with single mindedness throughout her career. Other dimensions of her life have been either subordinated to or absorbed within her career goals. Rather than wait for industry trends, she has acted to shape the world around her.

2. **Profound understanding of consumers and the industry environment.** Madonna has developed her strategy through a deep and insightful appreciation of customers and the music industry. Critical to her continuing success has been a deep understanding of the ingredients for sustaining popular appeal. The frequent re-invention of her style and sound has reflected an acute awareness of changing styles, social norms and attitudes in a fast clock-speed industry.

3. **Leveraging competences and addressing weaknesses.** Madonna has been able to exploit her abilities to develop and project her image and to exploit emerging trends, while protecting areas of weakness. Her weaknesses have been more than compensated for by her use of an extensive network of support personnel, including musicians, technologists, producers, dancers and designers. Her personal relationships have often been important in building her career.

4. **Consistent Implementation.** Without consistent implementation, even the best strategies are unlikely to succeed. Madonna has surrounded herself with individuals and organizations that have enabled her to deliver upon her vision. Through her various companies, such as Maverick, she built organizations that allowed effective marshalling of resources and capabilities, and quick responses to changes in the competitive environment.

5. **Continuous Renewal.** A key ingredient of Madonna's success has been her ability to renew her popularity again and again. She is known as the "queen of re-invention" within industry circles. Compare her abilities in re-invention to many "one-hit-wonders" in the music industry, or to performers such as the Rolling Stones who have enjoyed long periods of success, but whose fan-base has aged or remained largely unchanged.

Additional Literature

Anderson, J. and Kupp, M. (2006) Madonna: Entrepreneurship on a Dance Floor, *Business Strategy Review*, **17**(4): 26–31.

Anderson, J. and Kupp, M. (2006) Retail Financial Services in Germany, *ESMT Case Study*.

Anderson, J. and Kupp, M. (2008) MLP AG, *ESMT Case Study*.

Anderson, J. and Kupp, M. (2008) Virgin Mobile UK, *ESMT-TiasNimbas Case Study*.

http://www.forbes.com/lists/2009/53/celebrity-09_The-Celebrity-100_Rank.html

Grant, R.M. (2002) *Contemporary Strategy Analysis: Concepts, Techniques and Applications*, Oxford: Blackwell Publishers Inc.

MTV, Madonna Full Biography, http://www.mtv.com/music/artist/madonna/artist.jhtml

Popkin, H.A.S. (2006) Just call Madonna the recycled-Material Girl, *MSNBC*, 11 October 2006. http://www.msnbc.msn.com/id/15200899/

Porter, M.E. (1996) What is Strategy? *Harvard Business Review*, November–December.

Schmidt, V. (21 April 2008) Madonna goes to No. 1 for the 13th time, *The Times Online*, 21 April 2008 http://entertainment.timesonline.co.uk/tol/arts_and_entertainment/music/article3789058.ece

Shewan, D. (2008) Madonna Debuts Hard Candy, *Rolling Stone*, 1 May 2008.

Staff Writer (1992) Madonna is America's Smartest Business Woman, *Business Age*, June 1992.

Staff Writer (2005) Madonna on the dance floor, *The Sunday Telegraph*, 29 August 2005.

Staff Writer (2009) The Celebrity 100, *Forbes Magazine*, 3 June 2009.

The Times Online, http://entertainment.timesonline.co.uk/tol/arts_and_entertainment/music/article3789058.ece

Wing, R.L. (1988) *The Art of Strategy: A New Translation of Sun Tzu's Classic The Art of War*, trans, New York: Doubleday.

www.madonnafanclub.com

www.maverickrc.com

www.wikipedia.com

CHAPTER 2

Titian
Master and Intruder: Historical Perspectives on Strategic Innovation in the Venetian Art Market of the 16th Century

Introduction

Strategic innovation is the discovery of a fundamentally different strategy or way of competing in an existing industry. As discussed in Markides (1997) strategic innovation takes place when a company identifies *gaps* in an industry positioning map, goes after them, and these gaps grow to become big markets. These gaps have been identified as: (a) a *new* WHO – customer segments emerging or existing customer segments that other competitors have neglected; (b) a *new* WHAT – customer needs emerging or existing customer needs not served well by other competitors; and (c) a *new* HOW – ways of promoting, producing, delivering or distributing existing (or new) products/services to existing or new customer segments.

It has been shown that successful strategic innovators are most successful when they invade existing markets either by introducing products or services that emphasize radically different value propositions to those emphasized by established competitors, or by adopting radically different value chain configurations to those prevailing in the industry. Not surprisingly, the more innovative the strategy that a new entrant adopts relative to established firms, the higher the probability that the challenger will succeed.

In this chapter it is demonstrated that strategic innovation is not a new concept, but has deep historical roots. While the vast majority of research on strategic innovation has focused on firm strategies over the past two decades, we step back several centuries to discuss strategic innovation in the art world of Venice in the 16th Century. We first provide a description of how the Venetian art market evolved over a period stretching more than a century, and then discuss how the artist Tintoretto was able to create new market space in a "mature" industry dominated by the grand art master Titian. Subsequently, we reflect upon the lessons for modern firms from the innovations adopted by Tintoretto in attacking the Venetian art establishment some 500 years ago.

The Rise of Venice

Between the 9th and the 12th Centuries Venice became a city-state. Its strategic position on the Adriatic Sea made Venice's naval and commercial power almost invulnerable. A centre of the spice and silk trade the city developed into a flourishing trade hub with business relations extending far into the Byzantine Empire and the Islamic World. Venice achieved imperial power through its support of the fourth crusade, which ultimately led to expansion of the city-state's realm of political influence. The Doge Enrico Dandolo (1107–1205) strategically led the crusade to the Byzantine Empire and conquered Constantinople in 1204. He founded the Latin Empire, expanded the sphere of influence and thus achieved the first peak of Venetian power and wealth. At the peak of the 4th crusade the city employed 36,000 sailors, operated 3,300 ships and dominated Mediterranean commerce.

The political structure of Venice was underpinned by trade and commerce. The "Great Council" was the core governmental institution of Venice, and was elected by Venice's most influential families. The Great Council appointed all public officials and a Senate consisting of 200–300 members. The Senate elected the Council of Ten, and this secretive group directed administration of the city-state. One member of the great council was elected "Doge", or Duke, the ceremonial head of the city endowed with executive power.

The political and economic conditions of the 16th Century provided the foundations for a flourishing art market in Venice, with the city-state's great wealth and desire for status leading to massive investment in public buildings and grand palaces. There was extravagant competition among prominent Venetian families to demonstrate their wealth and status. Venice regarded itself as a political institution on the same level as the Emperor in Augsburg and the Pope in Rome, and, therefore, architecture and the arts in Venice were not only an expression of culture. Architecture and art in Venice had a functional purpose for the Great Council – to emphasize the status of the city-state as equal to any other power base of the time.

Technical Innovations in the Venetian Art World

In the 15th Century the Dutch painter Jan van Eyck (1390–1441) developed viable oil painting technology which had first been explored some 100 years before. In this technique the colour pigments were mixed with oil to a consistent creamy paste. Prior to the emergence of oil painting artists had used egg tempera technique (a mixture of egg, oil and water) for almost a thousand years. The new technology allowed artists to finish paintings in a much more precise and controllable manner and was perfect for workshop production. Furthermore, the new oil-based colours needed much more time to dry (sometimes a year) and so artists were able to mediate the neighbouring parts of a painting to a much higher grade by wet in wet painting technique or by applying thin layers of colour on top of each other. Some artists used more than 150 layers, thus creating a soft and very natural impression. Leonardo da Vinci's (1452–1519) *Mona Lisa* (1505) gives a perfect example of the mastership of this new way to paint. Oil technology had a fresh, natural and "modern" appearance in those times and offered new opportunities and different ways to produce artworks.

By being able to divide the painting process in clear working steps, prominent 16th Century painters started to establish workshops where they produced artworks supported by assistants. The workshop principle of a team of artists led by a "master" had been adopted earlier to complete major fresco projects in churches. The complicated production process of fresco, requiring preparation of the walls for the painting process, the transmission of studio drafts by puncture technology (the drafts, painted on cardboard were pierced with needles to the fresh and wet stucco), the just-in-time preparation of colours and so on, needed teamwork and meticulous organization.

With the evolution of oil painting technology, some prominent artists transmitted the teamwork and organizational approaches of fresco projects to satisfy growing demands in the art market being generated by the aristocratic class. Venetian aristocrats demanded grand portraits or mythological scenes in order to furnish their palaces in Venice itself, or for their summer villas on the mainland.

Different to fresco projects, it became possible for the art master to work on various projects at the same time by utilizing the long drying process of oil paint. Under the evolving workshop structure assistants were responsible for different steps in the production process. Some specialist assistants built stretched canvases and prepared the painting ground with a mixture of chalk and glue. Others prepared the colour, rubbed the colour pigment and mixed it with oil. More artistically skilled assistants transferred the conceptual sketches of the artwork, done by the master, to the canvas, and painted the background, executing less important parts of the composition. The master himself was responsible for controlling the process and painting the critical pieces of the composition, for example the faces or important people like the sponsor of the artwork, or well-known city vistas. Besides the calculable technical production steps, the new technology allowed painting on bigger formats compare to the artworks painted on wood. Furthermore, these artworks were transportable whereas earlier grand artworks had typically been commissioned for a specific building.

One of the most famous examples of this new kind of art form from the 16th Century, and which displayed the enormous potential of the newly developed stretched canvasses, was the The Ascension of Maria (the so called Assunta), painted by Titian for the Frari Church in Venice. Measuring 3.9 × 6.9 metres, the Assunta represented a format that had never been seen before in the art world.

There were also economical reasons driving the expansion of the production of large paintings on canvas; many churches had to be furnished with paintings in order to cover the walls (mostly side walls) of the architecture. Painting on wood was very expensive and simply not suitable for the big decoration projects of the time. Stucco technique was also too costly for minor parts of the church, and was susceptible to dampness caused by the high humidity of Venice. Oil paintings of the Venetian masters offered (relatively) good value for money, were resilient to humidity and transportable.

The Rise of Venetian Colourism

The Venetian art market was also famous by the 16th Century for the quality of its artists' colour composition which had been developed over several centuries. The special situation of Venice, surrounded by water, created a unique and specific light. In the full sun of midday colours started to fade, while in the shadows or the reflections of the city's waterways and canals the colours tended to have a warm intensive atmosphere. This environment required a very advanced understanding of the use of colours, and the Venetian artists became famous across Europe for their ability to work with the colour spectrum. Venetian artists differentiated themselves from competitors, for example artists working in Rome, and were able to establish their specific use of colours as an important "brand" factor. Bellini was one of the first Venetian artists to gain wider European recognition, and he was followed by artists like Giorgione, Veronese or Titian. Standing on the shoulders of the Venetian masters who had preceded him, it was Titian who developed the strongest understanding of colour composition that influenced many artists until the end of the 19th Century. The reputation of the Venetian artists for colour was so strong that artist's like the German Albrecht Dürer (1471–1528) travelled to Venice (1505–1506) in order study the grand masters of "Colorit".

It was not only a cultural shift and the development of technological innovations that helped the art market to blossom in Venice during the 16th Century – it was also the emergence of the commercial and political power of Venice. Other city-states like Rome and Florence were strong business competitors to Venice, and the city's huge investments into the arts might today be interpreted as an early form of city-state marketing. The city-state of Venice needed grand paintings in order to underline its political and economic status, and this need underpinned the development of the arts throughout the 16th Century. Quite a number of Venetian artists, like Titian, Veronese, Giorgione and Pordenone served this demand, and in doing so influenced generations of artists who followed them.

Emergence of the Grand Master

Illustrious Doge! Dear superior Sirs! From my childhood on I, Titian of Cadore, tried to learn the mastery of art, not out of cupidity, but more to gain for some glory . . . And though I was asked in the presence of his Holiness the Pope and other important Sirs empathically to join and serve them, I always had as an illustrious subject the wish to bequeath a monument to this famous city

—From a petition of Titian to the Council of Ten 1513

Titian (1490–1576) is widely accepted as the dominant master of the Venetian art world at the height of the city-state's rise. Deeply rooted in the famous Venetian Colourism school, Titian's style increased the dynamic use of colours dramatically compared to paintings from earlier periods. Titian had been an apprentice of Giovanni Bellini (1430–1516) who was the leading artist of his time and was the Venetian states painter. From Bellini, who created the blueprint for the Madonna paintings in the Renaissance, Titian learned the delicate use of colours creating a warm and harmonious style and the interaction of colours creating an intensive compositional dramaturgy. He developed an early sense of competition and didn't miss opportunities to profile his self along newest artistic developments. The young Titian practiced such competitions, so called "duels", very early. He went so far to compete even against young and close artist friends like Giorgione (1478–1510). With him he worked in a redecoration project side by side in an artist partnership, painting the stucco waterfront façade of the burned (1505) German trade office (Fondaco dei Tedeschi). In 1507 he didn't hesitate to dispossess Bellini from his position as states painter later. Bellini died in 1516 and, thereafter, as his friend and great talent Giorgione died early, Titian had only very few rivals in the Venetian art market, one of them was Pordenone (1484–1539), who he met around 1520 and later Paulo Veronese (1528–1588).

Titian's rise as a well-known and very successful artist began in 1518 when one of the most incredible objects of artwork in the history of art was unveiled. The painting was a piece of artwork such as had never been seen before. The size of the canvas had the incredible format of 3.9 × 6.90 metres. Building such a format had been a technical invention in itself. The composition followed a new concept; instead of a static composition Titian divided the painting into two parts. The lower part showed the group of Apostles holding their hands towards Maria. Above the Apostles a blue-sky separated them from the next level of the painting, where Maria emerged in a circle that consisted of clouds, little angel figures and an image of God at the top. The only bridge between these two, not physical but more spiritual levels, was the hand of an Apostle nearly touching the circle of clouds where Maria was positioned, and a little angel touching the head of one of the Apostles.

In this early cornerstone of his work Titian created a sophisticated interpretation of the religious topic. The viewer could switch perspective and so his or her understanding of the artwork. In one moment, starting to observe the painting from the bottom, it looks as though the Apostles lift Maria to heaven and to the area of God, and therefore she needs them to transform herself. With a different view, starting to observe the painting from the top, it looks like Maria and God emerge to the Apostles. In this perspective the Apostles need Maria to become aware about themselves and their spiritual role in the world.

This ambivalent construction and unique way to tell the biblical story was new. When the painting had been delivered to the Church's Franciscan monks they were sceptical about the radical new approach presented by Titian – the huge size of the canvas, the brilliant colours and the freedom of the composition. Only when an ambassador of the emperor came and asked to buy the painting and to forward it to Vienna did they decide to keep it. Titian's success with *The Ascension of Maria* was helped by his mastery of new technology and production processes.

With the wide acclaim of this outstanding painting Titian was able to build a dominant position in the Venetian art world that lasted for more than 60 years. Titian was THE portrait painter of his time, and served clients belonging to the highest level of society.

Artist for the Nobles

There was nearly no person of a high rank, neither princes nor noble ladies, whose portrait Titian was not painting; in that part of his art work he was an absolutely unequalled master

—Vasari, Art Historian, 1568

From the moment he had finished the *Assunta*, Titian's fame spread among the political and religious leaders of his time. There were very close relations between the power centres of Venice, Rome, Naples, Ferrara, Madrid and Augsburg, and in 1530 he started to paint for the Emperor Karl V. This royal patronage lasted for 26 years, and helped Titian to establish relations with nobles of other wealthy states. During the last 26 years of his life (1550–1576) the artist worked mainly for Philipp II, the son of Karl V who followed his father to the throne.

The outstanding reputation of Titian and his unique connections with both emperors is evidenced through the following story: Once Titian painted Karl V and his brush fell to the floor during the portrait sitting. To the astonishment of the members of his royal suite, the Emperor knelt down to pick up the painter's brush and paid in that way the highest deference to the old master. Titian's business relationship with Karl V and Philipp II established his reputation, and during his long career he worked for a great number of significant and well-known aristocrats, politicians and representatives of the Church. He painted the likenesses of the Doge of Venice, the Farnese Family of Ferrara, the Pope Paul III and many other prominent figures of the time.

Titian's artistic brilliance attracted all of these nobles, as he was able to create a kind of meta-reality of the portrait person. Titian's portraits did not simply display the image of the subject in an incredibly realistic way, but he was also renowned for being able to capture the human essence of the person and thereby add an emotional factor to his portrait painting. His artist friend Pietro Aretino wrote in a letter to the emperor Isabella of Portugal in 1537: "The whole world loves Titian, his style inspires the portraits with life, and nature itself hates him, because he instils the living person with his artificial spirit".

Given Titian's status, and the closed circle of aristocratic clients who dominated patronage of Venetian arts, it is perhaps not surprising that it was difficult for any other artist to challenge his position as THE grand master of Venice. There were only two options for working on grand art projects in Venice during Titian's time. One was to join the workshop of Titian by working as an assistant. The other almost unimaginable option was to work in a way that challenged Titian, a feat that was achieved by a young artist upstart named Tintoretto.

The Unorthodox Intruder – Tintoretto

Tintoretto (1519–1594) is probably one of the most ambiguous figures of the 16th Century Venetian art world. His radically unorthodox paintings cannot easily be classified. His manner of entering the market, in an environment with so many outstanding artists around him, was something never experienced before. In order to become part of the Venetian market Tintoretto chose a number of unorthodox strategic moves, in terms of his technical method, painting style, pricing model and approach to customers.

Born in Venice as the eldest of 21 children, Tintoretto was raised in the booming art world of his hometown. At the age of 15 his father took him to the studio of Titian to see whether he might be trained as an artist. A career as an artist seemed to be a rather promising one for a young person at the time, as the Venetian art market was booming. There was a huge demand for portrait work presenting the status of the Venetian aristocracy, as well as for grand projects to furnish the ever expanding architectural environment of Venice.

Tintoretto started his profession as a pupil of Titian, but remained as an assistant to the grand master for only ten days. Titian is reported to have expelled him from his studio because of the great talent that Tintoretto possessed, and because he was fearful of supporting the development of a potential future competitor. Furthermore, the drawings that Tintoretto completed in Titian's studio showed such great independence of manner that Titian was brought to the conclusion that the young Tintoretto would never be a proper pupil, willing to adapt his own style. Titian was absolutely right: within a decade Tintoretto would become one of his most serious rivals.

Later when Tintoretto was himself recognized as a master artist, he and Titian always kept a certain distance from each other. Nevertheless, Tintoretto remained a professed and ardent admirer of Titian.

Prestezza – A New Way to Paint

After his ejection from Titian's studio, Tintoretto embarked upon his independent career by exhibiting his paintings on Rialto Bridge, not hesitating to copy the style of his rivals. Rather than positioning his work as high art, he offered his ability to paint as a form of craftsmanship and became accustomed to meeting the demands of a wide spectrum of customers. From the very beginning he learnt to adapt his art to customer demands and economic capacity, and had minor commissions including furniture paintings, façade frescos and even minor jobs for the trade organization of the Fishmongers.

Right from the beginning and through the pressure of competition Tintoretto developed an innovative painting technique. It was different from the traditional style and enabled him to paint much faster than his colleagues. His quick painting method, called "Prestezza" followed three general steps. At first the artist applied a brown undercoat, using a colour that was used for etching technology, on the canvas. Thereafter he made a rough drawing using white colour, very often like a sketch. Then the actual painting process started.

Contrary to the technique of Titian that involved painting many layers of thin colour, Tintoretto used a "rougher" way of painting, sometimes working with broad brushstrokes. In many of his paintings the original undercoat shines through and is in that way part of the artwork. This innovative technique, combining the drawing quality of Michelangelo and the luminous quality of Titian's use of colour, created a new artistic style.

Many other artists and art critics, like the Venetian art scholar Vasari, were very ambivalent about Tintoretto's technique. Compared to the mature style of Titian, they saw a lack of quality and sometimes reacted quite negatively because, according to them, Tintoretto was destroying the high reputation of art and eroding the price structure of the market with his cheaper art production.

There was an economic rationale for the speed of Tintoretto's painting technique. Contrary to his wealthy competitor, Tintoretto was poor at the beginning of his career. In order to make a living he pursued customers who could not afford the price and status of Titian: and this is one of the reasons why it is possible to this day to find so many Tintoretto paintings in Venice.

While Titian started his career with a well-paid contract painting frescos at the Fondamente Tedesco together with his famous colleague Giorgione (1478–1510), Tintoretto started his career out in the streets selling early works in places like Ponte Rialto, the famous Venetian bridge. Tintoretto positioned himself in the market in a variety of different areas of art production, and didn't hesitate to paint and decorate house walls or furniture. He painted some of his early artworks for customers, even before they had asked him to produce them. This was an unusual approach at the time, and his willingness to produce in advance became a cornerstone in Tintoretto's business strategy. It can be seen as an early (and quite modern) "marketing" strategy to test products and stimulate the demand of new customers.

When he was offered his first contracts (his first prestigious commission came from a young Venetian patrician who ordered a set of 16 octagonal ceiling paintings in 1541), he accepted nearly every single commission, which put even greater pressure upon Tintoretto to develop fast painting techniques. During his long career, and in addition to many of his earlier minor pieces of work, Tintoretto produced more than 650 commissions for the Venetian market – more than twice the number of works of art completed by workshops of other Venetian painters, like Veronese, Titian or Pordenone.

Another business tactic, and a true cornerstone of Tintoretto's success, was that he offered paintings well below the price level of other prominent artists, and especially Titian. It was an approach that was both determined by and reflected in the growing demands of Tintoretto's customers, who tended to be drawn from the patrician rather than aristocratic classes. Instead of risking direct competition with Titian, who had an established reputation and was able to constantly raise the prices of his paintings, Tintoretto maintained the prices of his own workshop at an affordable level.

Radical Compositions

There were other compelling reasons driving Tintoretto along his path towards finding an innovative and differentiated role as painter. Direct competition with Titian for portrait commissions amongst the Venetian aristocracy was almost pointless, as Titian was acknowledged and highly sought after. Hence, Tintoretto had to make a significant difference in his own artistic style in order to win new customers and push their demand.

During his career Tintoretto became a leading figure in developing the Mannerism style in the Venetian art market. Influenced by Michelangelo, his figures showed a lot of abbreviations. Furthermore, he did not hesitate to show two different chronological aspects of a story in one painting. In the artwork *Presentation of the Virgin in the Temple* (1552/53), painted for the church Madonna dell Orto, Tintoretto had the genius to display the story twice in one painting. The little Maria is visible in three different situations. Firstly, when she is brought by her parents Anna and Joachim to the temple (Joachim stands at the left corner of the painting, Anna sits on the right corner of the painting, holding Maria), secondly, when Anna shows her daughter the way up the stairs to the priests, thirdly when she stands in front of the group of priests. The triple image of Maria is a very unique and visionary idea. Not before the invention of film during the early 20th Century did artists create the idea of "multi images" in single artworks.

But the *Presentation of the Virgin in the Temple* is also unique in other ways, and a good example of how Tintoretto systematically occupied market niches. The painting was created for the side chapel of the church in a very high position, about 5 metres above the floor. It could be seen only from a low distance of 4–5 metres. Mounting a painting, measuring 4.29 × 4.80 metres at such a height required a new solution in composition and perspective, as the viewer stands practically below the painting and looks far up. The bottom of the staircase is extended from the left to the right side of the painting and from there narrows to the upper part of the painting quiet dramatically. Tintoretto displayed the figures sitting and standing left and right of the staircase so dexterously that he created a pull effect that drew the viewer right to the top of the painting and its most important part where Maria is acknowledged by the priests.

Tintoretto's approach to be similar and at the same time different to his competitor Titian was very visible in the *Presentation of the Virgin in the Temple*. The warm golden and red colours Tintoretto used were a deliberate reference to the favoured palette (choice of colours) and technique of Titian, but the composition itself was a bold statement of Tintoretto in contrast to the original version of Titian, painted in 1534/38 for the Accademia. Through the use of dramatic perspective in Tintoretto's version, the viewer becomes literally a part of the painting. But in Titian's version the viewer is confronted with a static, self-contained horizontality, where one looks more from the outside and observes the situation pretty much like a stage.

The paintings of Tintoretto were so spectacular that they were widely discussed in Venice at the time. His work divided even his own customers into two groups of admirers; on one side were those who saw links to the mature technique and solidity of Titians artworks, while on the other side were those who revelled in his controversy and brave new techniques.

From this description it becomes clear that both the technique and the artistic style of Tintoretto made him unique in the Venetian art world. His way of painting led him to eventually develop huge projects to furnish big architectural projects in Venice. The most spectacular project of Tintoretto's career was the complete decoration of the Scuola San Rocco (1564–1588).

An Unfamiliar Business Tactic

Tintoretto moved progressively up-market throughout his career, and eventually challenged Titian for projects which the Grand Master might have considered to be at the low-end of his own elite market. The break-through for winning major commissions happened for Tintoretto in 1564. In that time the economic life in Venice was mainly organized in the so-called "Scuole". These organizations played a significant political role. For reasons of social and economical influence it was important to be a member of such an organization, but they had strict membership rules. One of the most famous was the "Scuola Grandi of Venice" that was founded in 1478 dedicated to the plague saint, San Rocco.

The Scuola Grandi of Venice built a representative building in the period 1516–1550 which was perfectly suited for a great scheme of pictorial adornment. In

1560 the Scuola invited Tintoretto and three other principal painters for a competition. Titian did not participate as he was too heavily engaged with portrait commissions outside of Venice. The group of artists were asked to present trial-designs for the oval centre painting in the main hall. The topic was "The Glorification of Saint Rocco". While the other painters produced their designs in small format, Tintoretto had taken the original measurement (240 × 360 cm) of the oval, sketched a great canvas, and painted it with his usual rapidity. He did so without letting anyone know what he was doing, but ultimately made a great impression. Beside this clever tactic Tintoretto referred heavily in his painting to the famous *Assunta* of Titian. The structure of the composition, with the emergence of God at the top of the painting and the vibrant use of colours, was close to Titian's painting. But, different to Titian, Tintoretto painted the topic in a far more modern way, using the baroque technique of abbreviation quite extensively.

The morning when the commission of the Scuola assembled to look at the different designs and to make their award, they found that Tintoretto had completely finished the work and had placed it in the position where it was planned for, at the centre of the ceiling. The angry reaction of the commission, saying that they had asked Tintoretto for a first design and didn't commission him to execute the work, was answered by the artist, that this was his method of making designs and that he didn't know how to proceed in any other manner to fulfil the demands of the competition. Further he claimed that designs and models of work should always be delivered in this way, so that no one could be deceived by a result different from the first design. Tintoretto closed his presentation with the offer that if the Scuola would not pay him for his labour, then he would gift the artwork to them. The painting is still in its place today.

The other competitors protested about such an "unfair" approach, and withdrew from the competition, with Tintoretto thereby obtaining the commission of the Scuola by default. He knew that the donation of the painting, dedicated as it was to the saint San Rocco, could not possibly be rejected. Furthermore, he offered all paintings for the remainder of the building at half of the normal price. In return for his generosity, he wanted to be accepted as a member of the Scuola.

This radical strategy turned out to be highly successful, with the Scuola proving Tintoretto with full membership status. Tintoretto then set to work decorating the entire building of the Scuola and the church of San Rocco next to it. The Scuola San Rocco is widely acknowledged as the most spectacular project of Tintoretto's career. It also delivered his desired outcome – to be accepted as a member of the Scuola, knowing this would help to increase his reputation as an artist and citizen of Venice.

Tintoretto's unorthodox pricing approach meant that he had a much wider range of commissions than Titian (or other artist colleagues). For example, in 1583 he painted an altar artwork for a wealthy client for which he was paid 400 Ducats. In the following year he worked for the Scuola of the linen weaver traders and delivered a painting for only 20 Ducats. Tintoretto's business manners using a price range or letting the customer decide about the sum in question was in full accordance with the habits of other Venetian artists or craftsmen. But the way he understood and handled this widely used practice was far more aggressive than the behaviour of any other prominent Venetian artist of his era.

A painting commission for the Doge's Palace completed by Tintoretto towards the end of his career in 1592 provides an insight into his radical approach to pricing. When he was asked to name his price, Tintoretto differed to the Palace authorities, knowing that they would pay him appropriately. But even when the buyers announced a considerable amount, Tintoretto refused a part of it. This not only helped to reinforce his humility, but also contrasted his own approach with that of Titian who was sometimes accused of greed. Tintoretto's approach to pricing irritated and upset many artist contemporaries who claimed that he was ruining the reputation of the arts and spoiling price levels. But his business manner can also be interpreted as an aggressive way to compete, and one might also assume that Tintoretto was well aware that he was growing the *total* art market.

Innovation Loops

Tintoretto started his art career with small decoration projects, and stepped slowly into real patronage with (primarily) patrician clients who ordered smaller paintings to furnish parts of their houses. When the Scuole projects became a stronger part of his business they provided him an entry to bigger commissions. These up-market moves called for innovation, and Tintoretto's "Prestezza" technique was developed, redesigned and tested in progressively more complex commissions. Compared to Titian who painted only a handful of huge paintings such as the *Assunta*, the oeuvre of Tintoretto contained dozens of large-scale paintings.

Even if Tintoretto was innovative in terms of technique and style, he did not claim artistic invention in every single painting. In many artworks he re-combined figures and compositions from his other paintings and did not hesitate to use similar compositions to competitors. This behaviour was part of his business approach – offering clients something familiar to his rivals, but still in his unique style and at a reasonable price. There were portraits in Tintoretto's work, but portrait painting was not his core business. In this field he was a direct competitor to Titian and he was not able to compete with the grand master's reputation.

Titian's Response to Tintoretto

Despite Tintoretto's fame later in his career he still stood in the shadow of Titian. Not before Titian died was Tintoretto appointed as state painter of Venice. Indeed, Titian was relatively successful in defending his dominance against the rise of Tintoretto, and he responded in many ways to his audacious rival.

Titian's very first act of defence had been expelling the teenage Tintoretto from his workshop. Titian had seen the incredible potential of the young artist and tried to cut off learning opportunities to distance the potential challenger from the reputation of his own studio. From that time Tintoretto had been forced to build his own career, and during the early years of exhibiting his paintings on the street and offering his artistic talent as craftsmanship, he did not challenge the grand master. By quickly expelling him from his workshop, Titian successfully prevented Tintoretto from becoming known to the nobility for whom he was painting. As evidence of this, the very few portraits out of the work of Tintoretto show customers mostly from the lower echelons of Venetian society.

Another effective tactic to control the high-end of the market had been Titian's very close relationship to the influential writer Pietro Aretino (1492–1556). With his sophisticated ability to write Aretino had access to the highest ranks of the nobility in Venice, like the Doge Andrea Gritti. Aretino was feared for his writing, and he could be described as one of the first society journalists. He had the power to argue for or against people and didn't hesitate, for example, to write a satiric treatise against the Pope in Rome. During the upcoming career of Tintoretto there was a widely held discussion about the quick painting technology Prestezza of Tintoretto. Many in the art establishment had been suspicious about the technique, because they thought it cheapened the reputation of art. These critics favoured the "mature" Venetian style of Titian, and Aretino was one of the prominent supporters of his friend the grand master.

Aretino had spoken badly of Tintoretto. But when both met one day Tintoretto invited Aretino to his studio to have his portrait done. During the sitting the painter suddenly pulled out a dagger from his robe. The surprised Aretino believed he was seeking revenge, and cried out and asked what he wanted.

Tintoretto replied coldly, "Don't move. I am taking your measurements." Suitably intimidated by the incident, Aretino never again spoke badly of Tintoretto and they ultimately became friends.

Aretino had been dead almost four years by the time Tintoretto was able to win the commission for the Scuola san Rocco. And it took more than ten years after Titian's death for Tintoretto to achieve the commission for the "crown" of his work, the huge *Paradise Scene* in the great hall of the Doge palace that was completed in 1592.

Building the constant and very successful relationships with his most important clients, Karl V and Philipp II, also helped Titian control the high-end of the market, especially for commissions for local and international nobility. But it should be also recognized that in response to Tintoretto's success, Titian progressively withdrew from what might be described as mid-level contracts in the Venetian market where his challenger was particularly strong. Despite being invited, Titian did not participate in the competition for the Scuola San Rocco in 1560. Already in his 70s, he chose instead to focus his energy on lucrative projects for his royal patrons.

It could be argued that Titian lost market share to Tintoretto later in his career, but this loss of market share should be viewed in the context of a growing Venetian art market, especially for mid-level and minor projects where Tintoretto's innovations expanded overall demand. It should also be acknowledged that as state painter of Venice until his death at the age of 86, Titian kept the most important office an artist could have in the city-state – and his workshop remained a highly profitable venture throughout his career.

Conclusion

Previous research has shown that strategic innovation is a particularly effective strategy for small firms or newcomers in an industry. Because these firms have to compete against entrenched established competitors, they cannot simply attack head-on, hoping to "outcompete" their bigger rivals. They must employ "guerrilla tactics" to avoid head-to-head competition. Tintoretto's success in entering a "mature" Venetian art market in the 16th Century demonstrates the tactics that a new entrant can use to strategically innovate.

Tintoretto's first insight was the understanding that it was not only the aristocracy that wanted to consume art of high quality – he discovered a new WHO.

Patricians, Scuole and churches also demanded works of art, but were unable to afford the high prices of the grand master Titian. By seeing the potential of these over-served or non-consuming customers, he was able to create a new market space for his own work, and at the same time significantly broadened the overall art market.

Tintoretto also introduced a new WHAT – affordable but high quality works of art, with relatively short delivery times. Previously, high quality artwork involved refined style and significant expense, but through his mastery of Prestezza technology he educated customers to accept rough brushstrokes and a certain level of artistic abbreviation, but compensated through the enhanced use of vibrant colours at significantly lower cost. In doing so, he created new dimensions of value for customers who were willing to make tradeoffs and break from tradition. While this departure from the artistic and pricing status quo was derided by many of his contemporaries, the resulting value proposition was compelling for many art buyers.

For Titian, major commissions had come through personal connections and reputation that had taken years to develop. Tintoretto was able to fast-track his success through a new HOW – by flooding the market with a high number of very high quality works of art – even if these artworks had not been asked for by their intended recipients. His coup in winning the commission for Scuola San Rocco was indicative of his use of guerrilla tactics to build his visibility in Venice, and eventually led to his appointment as state painter of Venice after Titian's death.

Tintoretto also innovated along the HOW that was the traditional value chain of art production. Contrary to Titian who had a strict control over the outcome of his workshop, Tintoretto was more relaxed about his workshop's production and gave greater artistic freedom to his assistants in order to handle the enormous amount of production. He also eliminated certain steps in the painting process, and through this new technique was able to significantly reduce the time required to complete works of art. This also resulted in a new artistic style (the new WHAT mentioned above), thereby avoiding head-to-head competition with Titian's dominance of the Venetian portrait scene.

Titian's response to Tintoretto also provides relevant lessons for 21st Century firms. Titian delayed Tintoretto's rise to fame by excluding him from learning skills in his own workshop and closing any access to his established client base. He leveraged his relationship with the writer Pietro Aretino to undermine the credibility of Tintoretto's painting style amongst many within the Venetian art establishment, and used his political influence to exclude Tintoretto from the highest echelons of public position until well after his death. Titian increasingly avoided head-on competition with Tintoretto by focusing his efforts on serving the Venetian nobility and expanding his reputation with the wider European aristocracy – a demanding and status-conscious customer base with whom Tintoretto never truly gained acceptance. In summary, evidence suggests that Titian fought back to retard Tintoretto's growth as a competitor but at the same time focused on his core business of grand projects and portrait painting for the nobility to avoid head-on confrontation in market segments where his higher cost approach put him at a disadvantage.

TABLE 2.1 Strategic Innovation in 16th Century Venice – Tintoretto versus Titian

	Titian	Tintoretto
WHO	Targeted Venetian and international nobility and political leaders, major church projects and city-state projects commissioned by the Great Council.	Initially targeted the mass-market through street sales, before moving to develop the market for the Venetian bourgeois class.
WHAT	Painting as high-art to communicate status and power. Predominantly portraits of the aristocracy and political and religious elite such as the Doge of Venice, the Farnese Family and Pope Paul III.	Painting as a form of craftsmanship. Initially produced smaller paintings to furnish homes, before moving on to commissions including furniture paintings and façade frescos, and projects for minor churches and commercial organizations such as the Scuole.
HOW	Deeply rooted in the refined Colourism school. Artistic invention and uniqueness a key differentiator. Maintained strong control over the output of workshop assistants. Workshop geared towards low-volume, highly detailed portrait painting, with modest number of commissions completed each year. New business won through close personal ties and networks. High prices.	Developed the Mannerism school that leveraged new Prestezza technology. Did not claim artistic invention in every piece. Guided rather than dictated the artistic output of workshop assistants. Workshop geared towards low-cost, high volume production of a range of artworks. New business often won through unorthodox sales and marketing techniques. Spectrum of prices depending on client.

Source: Markides (1997)

Finally, the success of Tintoretto in 16th Century Venice might provide a lesson in humility for 21st Century managers. While Titian and Tintoretto always kept a certain distance from each other, Tintoretto remained a professed and ardent admirer of his rival the grand master, expressed in the inscription he placed at the entrance of his studio: *Il disegno di Michelangelo ed il colorito di Titiano* ("Michelangelo's drawing and Titian's colour").

Additional Literature

Charitou, C. and Markides, C. (2003) Responses to Disruptive Strategic Innovation, *Sloan Management Review*, **44**(2 Winter): 55–63.

Dobni, C.B. (2010) Achieving synergy between strategy and innovation: The key to value creation, *International Journal of Business Science & Applied Management*, **5**(1 January): 48–58.

Hetzer, T. (1969) *Titian Geschichte seiner Farbe*, Frankfurt am Main: Vittorio Klostermann Verlag.

Kim, C. and Mauborgne, R. (1997) Value Innovation: The Strategic Logic of High Growth, *Harvard Business Review*, January–February: 103–112.

Markides, C. (1997) Strategic Innovation, *Sloan Management Review*, **38**(3 Spring): 9–23.

Millson, M.R. (2008/2009) Wilemon, Designing strategic innovation networks to facilitate global NPD performance, *Journal of General Management*, **34**(2 Winter): 39–56.

Nicols, T. (1999) *Tintoretto: Tradition and Identity*, London: Reaction Books.

Wolf, N. (2006) *I, Titian*, Munich: Prestel Verlag.

CHAPTER 3

Hirst
The Shark is Dead – How to Build Yourself a New Market

Introduction

On the 15 and 16 of September 2008, more than four and a half centuries after the break through of Tintoretto, the British artist Damien Hirst broke all the rules of the art market. He bypassed conventional distribution channels – dealers and gallery owners – by directly partnering with Sotheby's auction house – and with their help successfully sold more than 200 pieces of his works. Sotheby's auctioned art works which were less than two years old, which was another break from tradition. Hirst earned more than £110 million from the auction – in the midst of a global economic crisis and on the same day that the Lehman Brothers Investment house collapsed. The auction deeply shook the confidence of the "established" art world, with some suggesting that Hirst's approach could ultimately undermine the historical role of art galleries in the marketing and distribution of high-end works of art. Through the Sotheby's auction Hirst became one of the world's wealthiest living artists, and he achieved this feat by challenging long-established traditions surrounding the meaning of art and the processes and structures of the art industry itself.

In the two decades leading to the Sotheby's auction Hirst's work had focused upon the processes of life and death. His work was grouped into three broad areas: sculptures, paintings and glass tank pieces. His sculptures were most strongly represented by his cabinet series in which Hirst displayed collections of surgical tools or hundreds of pill bottles on shelves or even a life-size recreation of a chemist's shop. The paintings were divided into spot and spin paintings – spot paintings being randomly organized, colour-spotted saucer-sized discs, spin paintings being produced on a spinning table, so that each individual work was created through centrifugal force. The tank pieces typically incorporated dead and sometimes dissected animals – cows, sheep or sharks – preserved in formaldehyde. More recently Hirst had diversified into modern interpretations of Memento Mori artworks which were first created centuries ago.

In this chapter we discuss Hirst as an artist, businessman, entrepreneur and in-novator, and suggest that Hirst's rise to prominence should be understood in terms of his ability to be unhindered by established and preconceived norms of the art world – just as Tintoretto was able to innovate in Venice more than four hundred years before Hirst recognized that by the end of the 20th Century the established art world had become victim to a phenomenon that psychologists term "inattentional blindness" – when attention is very focused on specific tasks or approaches, humans often fail to perceive seemingly significant events or stimuli that can present either threats or opportunities. Hirst was able to smash the thick and opaque lenses of tradition in the established art world, and in do-ing so unleashed a blinding light of innovation. In turn, Hirst's innovative

---

TEXTBOX A – WHAT IS INATTENTIONAL BLINDNESS?

Imagine the following experience: you are searching for a free parking space on a busy Saturday morning. After driving around for 10–15 minutes, you eventually find a place to park the car. At work on Monday, your colleague asks why you snubbed her. She was waving at you from the pavement, but you seemed to look right through her. This is a phenomenon psychologists term "inattentional blindness" – when attention is diverted to a specific task, approach or process, humans often fail to perceive new stimuli. And it is this phenomenon of inattentional blindness that can lead even the most experienced managers to ignore opportunities to innovate – to identify new customer segments, to discover new products or services, or to invent new ways of delivering value.

---

approach saw the emergence of a new market space, a space in which he was the undisputed first mover and dominant brand. Throughout the chapter we draw upon lessons from Hirst for innovation in other established industries, and provide examples and case studies of contemporary firms that have managed to strategically innovate in their own market sectors.

Damien Hirst, the Bad Boy of Contemporary Art

Damien Hirst was born in Bristol in 1965. His father worked as a motor mechanic, his mother for the Citizens Advice Bureau. As a young man he applied for Leeds College of Art and Design, but was rejected. He then worked for two years on London building sites before studying at Goldsmiths College, University of London between 1986 and 1989.

After two years at Goldsmiths Hirst managed an independent student exhibition called *Freeze*. Hirst's own contribution was a sculpture, consisting of simple cardboard boxes painted with household paint. The show took place in the newly developed London Dockland site and was visited by Charles Saatchi, who was at that time one of England's leading art collectors and the co-founder with his brother Maurice of the global advertising agency Saatchi & Saatchi. In addition to his work in advertising, Charles Saatchi had become known worldwide as an art collector and owner of the Saatchi Gallery. Hirst established a professional relationship with Saatchi, a relationship that became an early cornerstone of his career.

After graduation, Hirst was curator at two "warehouse" shows: *Modern Medicine* and *Gambler*, together with his friend Carl Freedman. Again Saatchi visited the show and is reported to have stood open-mouthed when he looked at Hirst's first major animal installation *A Thousand Years*. This art-work consisted of a large glass case, containing maggots and flies feeding off a rotting cow's head. Maggots hatched inside a white minimal box, turned into flies, then fed on a bloody cow's head on the floor of a glass box. Hatched flies buzzed around in the box, many meeting their end in an electric insect-o-cutor; others survived to breed and continue the cycle. *A Thousand Years* was admired by renowned British artist Francis Bacon, who in a letter to a friend a month before he died, wrote about the experience of seeing the work. Margarita Coppack, an established art critic, noted that "It is as if Bacon, a painter with no direct heir in that medium, was handing the baton on to a new generation." Hirst had openly acknowledged his debt to Bacon, absorbing the painter's sometimes violent and bloody images and obsessions early on and giving them concrete existence in sculptural form. But through installations such as *A Thousand Years* Hirst made a very different art-statement to the work of Bacon, using living creatures as part of a sculpture for the first time.

The Saatchi Years 1991–2003

When Saatchi started his co-operation with Damien Hirst, he gave the Artist a "carte-blanche" and offered to fund whatever Hirst could produce. The result was presented in 1992 in the first "Young British Artists" show at the Saatchi Gallery. Hirst's first Saatchi-funded work was titled *The Physical Impossibility of Death in the Mind of Someone Living* and was a large shark in formaldehyde in a glass tank. The shark had been caught by a commissioned fisherman in Australia and had cost £6,000, with the total cost of production amounting to some £50,000. As a result of the show, Hirst was nominated for that year's Turner Prize, but it was awarded to Grenville Davey.

In 1993, Hirst's first major international presentation was in the Venice Biennale with the work, *Mother and Child Divided*, a cow and a calf sliced in halves and exhibited in separate glass tanks. He curated the show *Some Went Mad, Some Ran Away* in 1994 at the Serpentine Gallery in London, where he exhibited *Away from the Flock* (a sheep in a tank of formaldehyde). On the 9 May, Mark Bridger, a 35 year old artist from Oxford, walked in to the gallery and poured black ink into the tank, and re-titled the work *Black Sheep*. He was subsequently prosecuted, at Hirst's wish, and was given two years' probation. The sculpture was restored at a cost of £1,000.

With the full backing of Saatchi, Hirst's shows turned into ongoing successes and in 1995 he won the famous Turner Prize. This was the same year that New York public health officials banned the Hirst artwork *Two Fucking and Two Watching* featuring a rotting cow and bull, because of fears of "vomiting among the visitors", resulting in a storm of media coverage for Hirst's show in the United States. In 1997 the *Sensation* exhibition opened at the Royal Academy in London, and went on to a highly successful world tour. *A Thousand Years* and other works by Hirst were included. In 1998, his autobiography (at the age of 33) and art book, *I Want To Spend the Rest of My Life Everywhere, with Everyone, One to One, Always, Forever, Now*, was published. In 2000, Hirst's sculpture *Hymn* (which Saatchi had bought for a reported £1 million) was given pole position at the show *Ant Noises* in the Saatchi Gallery.

The professional relationship between Saatchi and Hirst began to unravel when, in April 2003, the Saatchi Gallery opened at new premises in County Hall, London, with a show that included a Hirst retrospective. Hirst disassociated himself from the retrospective to the extent of not including it in his CV, and was angry that a Mini car, which had been decorated for charity purposes with his trademark spots was being exhibited as serious artwork. The show also scuppered a Hirst retrospective that had been muted for London's Tate Modern. In response to the County Hall retrospective, Hirst accused Saatchi of being "childish" and declared: "I'm not Charles Saatchi's barrel-organ monkey . . . He only recognizes art with his wallet . . . he believes he can affect art values with buying power, and he still believes he can do it."

Following the schism between the two men, Hirst embarked on a mission to become more independent from Saatchi who still held a third of his earlier works. In September 2003 he had an exhibition *Romance in the Age of Uncertainty* at Jay Jopling's White Cube gallery in London, which made him a reported £11 million, bringing his wealth to over £35 million. It was reported that a sculpture, *Charity*, had been sold for £1.5 million to a Korean, Kim Chang-Il, who intended to exhibit it in his department store's gallery in Seoul. The 22 foot (6.7m) 6 ton sculpture was based on the 1960s Spastic Society's model, which is of a girl in leg irons holding a collecting box. In Hirst's version the collecting box is shown broken open and is empty.

Charity was exhibited in the centre of Hoxton Square, in front of the White Cube. Inside the gallery downstairs were 12 vitrines representing Jesus' disciples, each case containing mostly gruesome, often blood-stained, items relevant to the particular disciple. At the end was an empty vitrine, representing Christ. Upstairs were four small glass cases, each containing a cow's head stuck with scissors and knives. It has been described as an "extraordinarily spiritual experience" in the tradition of Catholic imagery.

In order to have more control over the manner in which his work might be exhibited and sold, Hirst bought back 12 works via Jay Jopling from the Saatchi Collection for a total fee reported to exceed £8 million. Hirst had sold these pieces to Saatchi in the early 1990s for a considerably lower price. In July 2004 Hirst commented about Saatchi, "I respect Charles. There's not really a feud. If I see him, we speak, but we were never really drinking buddies." The long-term and very successful relationship of Hirst and Saatchi came to an end.

The Years after Saatchi

After the separation from Saatchi, Hirst began to control and steer his own career. Provocation was the style for which he was known, but provocation as style created its own dilemma. As long as a provocation did not directly confront deeply held religious or political dogmas, Hirst understood the power of his art to draw attention without the risk of backlash. On 10 September 2002, on the eve of the first anniversary of the 9/11 World Trade Center attacks, Hirst said in an interview with *BBC News Online*:

> The thing about 9/11 is that it's kind of like an artwork in its own
> right . . . Of course, it's visually stunning and you've got to hand it to them
> on some level because they've achieved something which nobody would
> have ever have thought possible – especially to a country as big as America.
> So on one level they kind of need congratulating, which a lot of people shy
> away from, which is a very dangerous thing.

The next week, following public outrage at his remarks, he issued a statement through his company, Science Ltd:

> I apologise unreservedly for any upset I have caused, particularly to the
> families of the victims of the events on that terrible day.

Hirst came to understand that people become accustomed to provocation and shock, and that he had to find a way to give more credibility to his art-works. In order to establish and to assure a market, a well tested approach for an artist is to bridge their new art approach with relevant references from art history. An artist will be honoured and acknowledge for the renewal he is able to make, but for buyers to truly embrace an artist they must be reassured about the expected future value of their investments based on parallels to artistic peers and historical predecessors. It could be said that if it is the artist that breaks the rules, it is art history that establishes the continuity. This combination is the key to long-term success in the art market.

In December 2004, *The Physical Impossibility of Death in the Mind of Someone Living* was sold by Saatchi to American collector Steve Cohen, for $12 million (£6.5 million), in a deal negotiated by Hirst's New York agent, Gagosian. Cohen, a Greenwich hedge fund manager, then loaned the work to MoMA, New York. Sir Nicholas Serota had wanted to acquire it for the Tate Gallery, and Hugo Swire, Shadow Minister for the Arts, tabled a question to ask if the government would ensure it stayed in the country. But UK export regulations on works of art did not apply to living artists.

Following his split from Saatchi, Hirst seemed acutely aware of the need to anchor his reputation. This focus was supported by his friend and gallery owner Jay Joplin who encouraged Hirst to work on more ambitious art. In June 2006 Hirst exhibited alongside the work of Sir Francis Bacon (1909–1992) at the Gagosian Gallery at Britannia Street London. Along a series of triptychs of Bacon, Hirst showed among other works a new formaldehyde work entitled *The Tranquillity of Solitude* that was influenced by Bacon. Using the subtitle "For George Dyer", which was a reference to a famous triptych of Bacon, Hirst again connected his work with British tradition. Through this exhibition Hirst achieved an important step towards the established side of the market – customers could buy a piece of his artwork that combined both new and traditional themes.

For the Love of God – the Skull Project

In May 2007 Hirst made a new statement through his *Beyond Belief* exhibition at the White Cube gallery in London. The centre-piece of the show was a human skull recreated in platinum and adorned with 8,601 diamonds worth some £15 million, a production cost that stretched the boundaries of contemporary art production. Titled *For the Love of God*, the asking price for the skull was £50,000,000. It didn't sell outright, but on 30 August 2008 it was sold to a consortium that included Hirst himself and the White Cube gallery.

Hirst's skull project allowed him to innovate along two dimensions. Firstly, Hirst related his work to one of the most popular subjects of art history, namely the Memento Mori, but went far beyond any other Memento Mori object ever created in terms of expense and extravagance. Memento Mori artworks were first created as reminders of the mortality of human beings and had been very popular in the 18th and 19th Centuries, but rarely incorporated precious stones or metals. Secondly, after selling the skull to the consortium it was exhibited in one of the most well established homes of traditional art – the Rijks Museum in Amsterdam.

The whole Rijks exhibition of *For the Love of God* followed a well-planned marketing approach. The exhibition was advertised all over the city by posters, and at the museum itself the skull was presented in an extra room, right next to the icons of art history Rembrandt, Vermeer and other famous Dutch artists. Visitors had to wait in the Rembrandt room until they got permission to enter. After seeing *For the Love of God* they were guided to another exhibition room where the artist had arranged an exhibition around the topic Memento Mori by using classical artworks out of the depot of the Rijks Museum. All of the Memento Mori artworks were subtitled with comments of Hirst himself, positioning him as an expert at the same level as the curators of the museum.

Leaving the exhibition rooms, visitors passed through the museum shop where they were presented with a range of merchandise related to the Hirst exhibition. From T-shirts and badges, to posters and cups, Hirst provided a full range of products, making *For the Love of God* affordable for all budgets. The exhibition seemed a win–win situation for the artist and for the museum. Hirst received the full honour and affirmation of having exhibited in the Rijks Museum, while the Museum attracted thousands of new visitors.

The Dance Around a Golden Calf – the Sotheby's Auction

In mid-2008, Hirst announced the next unusual move, that was by-passing his established galleries for his next show *Beautiful Inside My Head Forever* in preference of Sotheby's auction house. The Gagosian Gallery, who had sold Hirst's work for 12 years, said they would attend to make bids to buy it, and said, "As Damien's long-term gallery, we've come to expect the unexpected."

The star items were *The Golden Calf*, an animal with 18-carat gold horns and hooves, preserved in formaldehyde, and *The Kingdom*, a preserved tiger shark; other preserved animals included a zebra and a "unicorn". The sale included spot and butterfly paintings, many incorporating gold and diamonds, that had begun to attract some attention from critics who questioned the degree to which these pieces were really Hirst's own work given his increasing use of production assistants. Hirst defended the practice claiming that the real creative act is the conception of art, not the production of art, and that as the progenitor of the idea he was therefore the artist.

By September 2008 some 21,000 visitors had viewed the items on offer at Sotheby's, with the actual auction restricted to 656 ticketed clients on the first night of the planned two-day sale. All 56 lots on offer on the first night were sold for a total £70.5 million, exceeding Sotheby's estimate of £65 million. The £10.3 million sale of *The Golden Calf* beat Hirst's previous auction record. *The Kingdom* sold for £9.6 million, more than £3 million above its estimate. The second day of the sale, taking place in the morning and afternoon, raised £41 million, making a sale total of £111 million ($198 million) for 218 items with three remaining unsold (two others were sold privately after the auction). The auction was successful beyond any expectations, setting a world record for a single-artist auction.

Lessons for Managers

Damien Hirst has, throughout his artistic career, broken the rules of the established art industry and his success provides a number of lessons for organizations. Much of the established theory and approaches to competitive strategy focuses on how a firm can analyse the dynamics within an established industry, and then develop an approach to position itself *within* that industry. There is a significant focus upon understanding established competition, and developing approaches to beat incumbent firms along dimensions such as lower cost or more differentiation. Equally, firms are encouraged to identify existing customer demand, and then to serve that demand faster or better than other firms. While these approaches are important, they can lead even the most experienced managers to ignore opportunities to create completely new market space. As we have discussed in our chapter on Tintoretto and the 16th century art market, for an organization to identify new opportunities for strategic innovation it needs to ask three interrelated questions as proposed by Markides (1997):

1.   WHO are the customers that we currently do not see?

2.   WHAT are the products and services that we are blocking from our consciousness?

3.   Are we blind to new ways of HOW we might operate our business?

One of Hirst and Saatchi's earliest breakthroughs was the recognition that the late 20th Century had seen the emergence of "non-traditional" art buyers – a new WHO that the contemporary art world of artists, dealers, curators and galleries had been slow to serve. These were consumers, many of them from the relatively new wealth of the Middle East, Asia and other emerging markets, who did not buy for pleasure alone – they invested and expected a good margin when they decided to sell the artwork again. Both Hirst and Saatchi understood that a very real issue for these buyers at the high-end of the art market was expected future return on investment – the degree of certainty with which a piece of artwork could be sold for a price higher than at which it was acquired. And the only way to deliver the certainty of expected returns was to create unique and strongly branded products.

One of Hirst's prominent customers, who understood the value of investment, was Steve Cohen, the billionaire who purchased Hirst's shark sculpture *The Physical Impossibility of Death in the Mind of Someone Living*. "The idea that the American hedge fund broker Steve Cohen, out of a hypnotized form of culture-snobbery, would pay an alleged $12 million for a third of a tonne of shark, far gone in decay, is so risible that it beggars the imagination", wrote the art critic Robert Hughes on 13 September, 2008, in the *Guardian*. "Of course, $12 million would be nothing to Cohen, but the thought of paying that price for a rotten fish is an outright obscenity." Even if one criticizes the amount of money paid for a shark (which started to rot meanwhile and was substituted by a new exemplar), Cohen was clear about the return of investment, as cultural recognition on the highest level, by donating the artwork to the MoMa museum.

This is an important notion to appreciate, the very careful and almost forensic look at potential instead of existing customers. Who are the customers that are under- or over-served by the existing market offers or not even thought of by the established market player? Think of MAN Ferrostaals approach to serve a new and up to then unserved customer segment, insurance companies and venture capital investors. MAN Ferrostaal is an internationally operating company providing industrial services and systems for the world market. Based on its decades of experience and supported by a worldwide network of subsidiaries and partners MAN Ferrostaal, acting both as general contractor or consortium member, specializes in the lump sum turnkey supply of petrochemical plants, metallurgical plants and facilities for the gas and crude oil industry. Traditionally customers in this industry are privately owned gas, oil or chemical producers or state-run companies.

MAN Ferrostaal identified the opportunity of a new customer segment when it was approached by Colonial Life Insurance Company (Trinidad) Limited CLICO. CLICO was looking for investment opportunities in Trinidad. MAN Ferrostaal as a general contractor and financial engineer designed a project, which involved planning, financing, running a methanol plant and eventually even marketing the products. MAN Ferrostaal was able to deliver value to this project not only by taking over the financing part but also by partnering and taking over ownership and therefore creating a brand new business model.

This was only possible through a common understanding and a very close partnership approach between MAN Ferrostaal as the general contractor, CLICO as their customer, PROMAN, a project management and construction company, and the Kreditanstalt fuer Wiederaufbau (KfW) who were responsible for the tailor made project-financing scheme. Today the transfer of the "Trinidad Model" to other markets is one of the MAN Ferrostaal core activities, and the company works actively to identify and approach insurance companies and venture capital investors around the world.

Another one of Hirst's early insights was his recognition of the fact that by the end of the 20th Century the established art world had come to define "works of art" rather narrowly. In the early years of Hirst's career both he and his collaborator Charles Saatchi identified the need to create a new WHAT – images, symbols and signs buyers could acknowledge as unique, whether or not they were attracted to them. This was a tactic Saatchi had refined through his experience as the head of an advertising company, and which fit perfectly with the extroverted and provocative potential of Hirst as an artist.

While animals – alive and dead – had been exhibited in museums, aquariums, zoological gardens and scientific exhibitions for centuries, the art world had remained largely blind to the potential of incorporating biological elements. Through his use of animals and animal parts in his sculptures and other objects of art, Hirst removed the blinkers of artistic tradition and created a uniquely differentiated artistic style. When Hirst organized the *Freeze* show as a young artist he said: "I can't wait to get into a position to make really bad art and get away with it. At the moment if I did certain things people would look at it, consider it and then say 'fuck off'. But after a while you can get away with things."

Hirst's shark sculpture became the icon of British art in the 1990s, and a symbol of Britart worldwide. Even if a shark could be seen in an aquarium or as a preserved specimen in a zoological exhibition, any artist attempting to replicate Hirst's concept would be seen as something akin to a conceptual plagiarist. Through the

For the Love of God project it appeared that Hirst was not only trying to relate his work closer to tradition – much more he was testing the boundaries of the market itself. Was it possible for the art market to accept a piece of new art that cost £15 million to produce – exceeding the cost of virtually any other art product up to that moment – for a list price of £50 million, an increase of 230 percent?

The degree of opposition to Hirst's work indicated the degree to which the established art world was blinkered to the massive commercial opportunities arising from the new WHAT created by Hirst and Saatchi during the 1990s. The leading art critic Robert Hughes had attacked Hirst as being responsible for "the decline of contemporary art" and well-known British politician Norman Tebbit commenting on Hirst's *Sensation* exhibition, wrote "Have they gone stark raving mad? The works of the 'artist' are lumps of dead animals. There are thousands of young artists who didn't get a look in, presumably because their work was too attractive to sane people. Modern art experts never learn." But Hughes, Tebbit and many other highly respected critics from the art "establishment" seemed blind to an emerging reality – at a time when the quantity of art being produced was exploding, successful commercial exploitation of art was no longer primarily about the communication of the inner meaning of the artist.

Hirst's idea was not first and foremost to produce a solid and sustainable body of work, like artists such as Paul Klee, Picasso or Barnett Newman. Even the modern production tactics of Andy Warhol and his factory or Jeff Koons did not appear to appeal to Hirst early in his career. Instead, the primary objective of Hirst seemed to be to establish his own brand through direct and often shocking provocation. What he proved, and what astounded many art critics, was that there was a multi-million dollar market for artwork incorporating rotting meat, maggots, dead sheep and all manner of other "unique" materials that stretched the boundaries of the meaning of art. The world of contemporary art had seemed to block the potential use of these materials from its collective consciousness.

As a company you will have to start with the same questions and observations. What does the customer really want? And is the customer able to talk about and express his needs? Asking customers is only one way to identify new products or services. Equally important is to develop a deep understanding of the customer's business and how the customer is satisfying its own customers' needs. In this way, a company can think ahead and identify new services to offer before the customer even thinks of them. And of course you can observe the customer, how is he using or not using your current products, adapt them to his environment and so on. Think of the Netherlands-based companies Douwe Egberts and

Philips that cooperated to bring to market one of the most successful coffee systems of all time – the Senseo.

In the mid-1990s Douwe Egberts suffered difficulties with the revenue of their cash-cow "Roodmerk" filter coffee. So the firm conducted market research among a representative group of coffee drinkers. Although the research showed that the end consumers liked the coffee, they also found out that three issues were mentioned with a remarkable frequency: the desire for a one-serving-principle, the preference for home consumption to be like an "out-of-home" experience and the wish for push-and-drink-convenience. These issues did not necessarily mean that the taste of coffee had to be changed, but that the way of drinking coffee and thus the Douwe Egberts customers' behaviour had changed. As Margret, one of the product managers at Douwe Egberts who was part of the team at that time remembers: "We already had a high quality coffee at hand. But we knew that we would only make a difference if we could serve this coffee to the new type of customer in a completely new way – a concept that would create a revolution in the market and be so different that at least for a few years Douwe Egberts would be the only company to serve the market with this concept".

While looking at the outcome of its market research, the marketing department of Douwe Egberts had the idea that there was an opportunity to create value by creating a new product (new WHAT). When elaborating on a concept that would link the results to a comprehensive picture of the product, they came up with a complete "coffee system", which they called Senseo. Designed in partnership with the home appliance division of Philips, the Senseo system was designed to heat water to the correct temperature, and dispense coffee after brewing using mild pressure and a special spray head that produced a unique frothy coffee layer. The layer resembled an espresso, thereby creating the sense of an "out-of-home" experience. The look of the machine also distinguished itself clearly from a regular coffee making machine, and was easy to operate with only 3 buttons to push for on/off and the selection of the type of coffee. Another unique feature of the coffee maker was that its water reservoir was detachable, making it easy to fill under the tap. This detachable water reservoir held up to 750 millilitres of water, permitting consumers to make 5 cups of coffee without a refill of the water tank. But the machine was only half of the system. The other half was the specially designed coffee pods. These pods contained a measured serving of coffee for one cup. The original Douwe Egberts Senseo coffee pods were available in mild, regular and dark roast as well as decaffeinated.

Through the development and launch of the Senseo system Douwe Egberts and Philips assumed that their customer base would grow; casual coffee drinkers would be attracted by the push and drink convenience, and the individual or 'lonely' coffee drinkers – those alone in the office or at home – might increase their coffee consumption as they were suddenly able to brew only a one-cup-serving. And the Senseo development team were right – the actual sales for the Senseo brewing systems crushed all expectations. Within 14 months of launch, some 2.2 million Philips Senseo appliances were sold, with subsequent sales averaging 2 million per year. With an average retail price of €80 this meant a yearly revenue on sales of systems of €160 million. For Douwe Egberts, the figures were also impressive: revenue on pod sales in the first year totaled more than €30 million, growing rapidly to annual sales of €100 million per annum within three years. By providing their customers with a new 'WHAT' – an integrated, affordable and user friendly home coffee system – Philips and Douwe Egberts were able to differentiate themselves from their competitors and reap substantial profits.

But Hirst did not only question the WHO and WHAT of the established art world. He also challenged established approaches to HOW artwork should be exhibited, produced and sold. Right from the beginning Hirst followed a different path to access art consumers. Instead of using only the traditional way of distributing art through dealers he also adopted the role of curator.

While in the past the role of the curator was to select and often interpret works of art by writing labels, catalogue essays, and other supporting content for an exhibition, this role was changing with the rise of artists organizing exhibitions, and with the emergence of curator-dealers who established their own private galleries. Hirst appreciated the new importance of the curator, especially the dealer-curator in a market that was lacking transparency and that was dominated by long-term business relationships. Understanding this trend, Hirst adopted a dual role by being at the same time a curator and an artist delivering pieces of artwork for his shows. While this concept was not entirely new, Hirst took it to a new level and played it differently.

Hirst's adoption of the role of curator appeared a response to the way in which power had shifted in the art industry. By the 1990s high-end contemporary art was traded in two main ways: through a 'primary' market of private dealers and dealer-curators that offered works coming directly from artists' studios through their own private showrooms, private galleries and at art fairs such as the Venice Biennale, Art Basel and London's Frieze Art Fair; and, through a 'secondary' market of both dealers and auction houses that offered the resale of art objects. Some primary dealers had also began to build secondary resale businesses for their favoured artists in the 'backrooms' of their showrooms and galleries. Key to a primary dealer's success was his or her ability to manage a complex two-sided network – on the one side were established or high-potential artists, and on the other a group of wealthy and influential collectors.

It was virtually unheard of for artists to offer their new works direct at auctions, and the secondary market of auctions and dealers focused on resale of the work of artists who had already established a reputation in the primary market. For auction houses and secondary dealers the key to success was obtaining high-quality works for sale, and they attracted sellers through their ability to market to a global network of collectors and gain high prices.

The rise of importance of prominent private dealer-curators such as London's Jay Jopling, owner of the White Cube Gallery, in influencing the primary market and defining the parameters of artistic talent constrained the ability of individual artists to build their own personal brands. Furthermore, an explosion in the number of trained and talented artists in the United Kingdom had meant that building reputation had become increasingly difficult. While ten to twenty years earlier primary market dealers had served artists in order to promote the unique aspects of their work, by the early 1990s the dealer-curator started to use artists to underline their own concepts and shape artistic trends through their own private galleries that were open to the public. In this way dealer-curators and prominent private galleries had become increasingly powerful in their ability to 'make or break' up-and-coming artistic talent.

The complex filtering process by which artists gained acceptance at the upper-end of the contemporary art market was termed by the industry as 'validation' and without the endorsement of prominent dealer-curators and private galleries; it was virtually impossible for young artists to be shown at leading art fairs or to be placed in a public museum of modern art such as the New York Metropolitan Museum of Art or London's Tate Modern – the ultimate stamp of approval. So in a market that was lacking transparency and that was dominated by long-term business relationship, there was a need to re-define the rules in order to create a new market space.

Understanding that an art exhibition could be leveraged as an artistic statement in itself, Hirst created branded exhibition concepts and used his artist colleagues to contribute and build upon his *own concept* of the show. Hirst understood that he had to re-define the rules in order to create a new market space. He did this by initiating shows as curator, and then leveraged these shows to 'validate' his own artwork – a novel approach that challenged established roles of both artists and curators.

Hirst created a new HOW in terms of art production. Much has already been written about Hirst's innovative use of "new" materials, especially animals, he also innovated with regard to methods of production. Although Hirst participated physically in the making of early works, he had always needed assistants. But by the late 1990s the sheer volume of work produced necessitated a "factory", with Hirst working closely with his main art production company called Science Ltd. While "factory" production had been used by other prominent artists throughout history, Hirst was perhaps unique in the minimal level of input that he contributed to many of his works. In 1999 Hirst had publicly said that he only painted five of more than 300 spot paintings himself because, "I couldn't be fucking arsed doing it"; he described his efforts as "shite" – "They're shit compared to . . . the best person who ever painted spots for me was Rachel [Howard]. She's brilliant. Absolutely fucking brilliant. The best spot painting you can have by me is one painted by Rachel." Speaking about the artistic value of his spin paintings in *Life and Death and Damien Hirst* he declared: "They're bright and they're zany – but there's fuck all there at the end of the day." Hirst once told a story about a painting assistant who was leaving and asked for one of his spot paintings: "I told her to make one of her own. And she said, 'No, I want one of yours'. But the only difference, between one painted by her and one of mine, is the money."

Hirst believed that modern-day artists had been largely blind to yet another new HOW – the sale of contemporary art through the world's auction houses. In mid 2008, Hirst announced the unusual move of by-passing his established primary dealers/galleries for his next show *Beautiful Inside My Head Forever* in cooperation with Sotheby's Auction House. This was a shock to primary dealers – for several decades the traditional model had been for primary dealers to sell to collectors, for collectors to (eventually) sell to auction houses, and for auction houses to sell to 'secondary' dealers who would then sell on to collectors or public galleries. 'Serious' primary market collectors would usually sell for one of three reasons – death, divorce or debt (known in the industry as the 3Ds). Primary dealers had a vested interest in building the careers of their stable of individual artists, while the auction houses and secondary dealers objective was typically to try to achieve the highest price possible.

Art has been 'consumed' for millennia, but by the turn of the new millennium it was possible to define three levels of art consumption – spectators, collectors and investors. Spectators appreciated art through public and private galleries but did not necessarily actively participate in the purchase of art works, especially at the high-end of the market. Collectors actively purchased and owned art for pleasure as a form of individual consumption, and could be profiled according wealth. High net worth individuals had always been an important segment of collectors, with 'new' collectors often coming from the ranks of the entrepreneurial nouveau rich and from emerging economies such as Russia, China and India. There had also been the emergence of what the industry termed the 'mass affluent' segment that purchased works of art for £3,000 or less. Investors, whether individual or institutional, purchased art as an alternative investment vehicle with an expectation to earn profit through the upward movement of art prices over time. Investors could seek long-term returns by holding on to an art object for years, or act in a more speculative way by 'flipping' an artwork soon after purchase for a short-term gain.

Collectors who bought in the primary market were typically those 'risk takers' excited by the prospect of picking up a potential masterpiece, or collectors who wanted preferential access to an established artist's output. Primary collectors who quickly 'flipped' their purchases for a profit at auction were viewed unfavourably, and could sometimes be excluded from future access to new works. Private dealers in the primary market typically gave preferential treatment to collectors who were willing to buy a large number of works by an individual artist, and this treatment often included direct access to the artists themselves, through artist's dinners or studio visits. Art is a product whose status is affected by the status or reputation of owners, so primary dealers had a vested interest in making sure a particular artist's work was placed correctly.

Primary dealers were particularly interested in placing works in public galleries of modern art, with the Metropolitan Gallery of Modern Art in New York as the ultimate judge of an artist's recognition, but with institutions such as the UK's Tate Modern and Centre Pompidou in France also increasingly influential. Recognizing their power and influence, public galleries were in a strong position to request 'discounts' from primary dealers. So the ideal buyer in the eyes of many dealers was a wealthy private collector who would pay full market price of an artwork, but who had expressed an interest in donating all or part of his or her collection to a respected public art museum. Gaining entry into a major public art museum represented not only recognition at the highest level for an artist, but also meant final repository for an artwork as later sale of artworks by leading public galleries was rare. In turn, this 'exit' of an artwork from the market increased the scarcity of works in circulation, thereby positively impacting future sales of the artist and primary dealer.

Collectors in the secondary dealer market tended to see the primary market as murky or time consuming, or were investors who liked the reassurance of a more transparent marketplace. But the role of secondary dealers had been eroding for some time, with end buyers in the secondary market becoming increasingly active in auction sales. Auction houses had also established private (i.e. non-auction) sales activities – in 2007 Christies made private sales of some $542 million, and Sotheby's of $720 million, with some industry analysts predicting that private sales could represent up to 20% of auction house revenues by 2010. Both Sotheby's and Christies had established advisory services for wealthy clients looking to strengthen their art portfolios, as had many private banks. Speaking about the Sotherby's auction Hirst said, "It's a very democratic way to sell art and it feels like a natural evolution for contemporary art. Although there is risk involved, I embrace the challenge of selling my work in this way." After the Sotheby's auction, Hirst implied in a number of interviews that he believed contemporary art had become over-priced – including his own work. At the end of 2008 contracts were renewed for only five of twenty-five assistants who had worked with Hirst at Science Ltd as the result of a planned termination of certain bodies of work, including medicine cabinets, as well as spin and butterfly paintings. Some art commentators claimed that this was in response to over-supply that had begun to negatively impact prices for some of Hirst's "mass-produced" artworks, and would almost undoubtedly boost the value of works in future auctions.

The fundamental question of how a company delivers value to the customer is very important and offers various ways for strategic innovation. Just reflect upon the distribution methods you use, the inventory methods, the manufacturing methods or the marketing methods. In each and every one of these dimensions you have the chance to break the rules of the game, come up with a radically different approach and therefore strategically innovate. Just think of zopa.com, a London based peer-to-peer lending platform. A good example of this approach has been the entry of Route Mobiel to the automotive road-side assistance market in the Netherlands. Route Mobiel was founded by entrepreneurs Michel Muller and Marc Schröder who were known in the Netherlands as "monopolist attackers". They had prior experience with entering into an established industry, and in 2000 had launched a chain of cheap self service petrol stations without employees under the Tango brand. By reducing cost adding elements, such as personnel, they were able to lower the price of gasoline and compete with established players. By 2004 there were more than 100 Tango branded petrol stations without any personnel.

Route Mobiel entered the Dutch market to challenge the virtual monopoly of the ANWB that had dominated the sector as a virtual monopoly for decades. Until 2004 the ANWB had never had a year in which it lost members, but after Route Mobiel's entry the association saw tens of thousands of members defect to the competition or simply discontinue their memberships. The new competitor primsed to offer road-side support with the "same quality" as the ANWB for a price that was 42% lower. To deliver this promise, Route Mobiel had a radically low-cost business model, with just ten full-time employees compared to an employee count of some 4,300 for the ANWB.

The automotive road-side assistance industry had been traditionally dominated by the ANWB, with no real nation-wide alternative existing for automobile drivers up until the mid-1990s. Basically, there had been three choices for road-side assistance: join ANWB as a member, call in on automotive support service via car brands (e.g. Volvo Assistance) or turn to a local garage owner. ANWB and some car brands were the service providers offering nation-wide automotive support service at the roadside. Out of 6 million cars in The Netherlands by 2004, some 4 million were registered as a member of ANWB.

ANWB's proposition to the customer was focused on a good level of service and quality, where they acted as a reliable and trustworthy party with years of experience in the automotive service support industry. The organization provided nation-wide coverage through an extensive network of roadside telephones and used in-house trained engineers to provide roadside service. The ANWB had 1,100 full service cars fitted with all kind of tools and spare parts. When having car trouble, the members contacted the call centre and a service vehicle would be directed by the call centre to repair the car on the spot. If the car could not be repaired, the ANWB would tow the vehicle to the nearest affiliated automotive repair centre. The ANWB contact centre focused on optimizing communications with customers, both on the phone and via e-mail. Over 1,000,000 phone calls and 300,000 emails were processed in 2003. Consumer research revealed that some 70% of ANWB members maintained a subscription primarily because of the broken-car-help service.

In addition to its basic roadside assistance and emergency services, the ANWB also owned Logicx, a 24 hours service for the transportation of broken cars and shortlease of replacement cars. This department worked closely with the ANWB Emergency Centre and had around 850 cars for short lease. The company also offered a range of automotive and non-automotive Insurance products sold by its insurance subsidiary Unigarant, and national and international travel services were offered through ANWB Travel. Publishing of the ANWB magazine, maps and other information materials was managed by the ANWB's Multimedia Publishing department (MMU), although demand for maps and other printed information had been steadily declining with the increasing uptake of affordable satellite navigation systems, the Internet and online tools such as Google Maps.

ANWB members also had access to ANWB Legal Services for assistance in automotive related legal cases. Driving lessons were offered through the ANWB's driving school ARO in competition with private driving schools.

When Route Mobile entered the Dutch market for roadside assistance services the company positioned itself very much as a low cost service provider focused exclusively on road-side assistance. The company offered basic automotive support service at a rate of €50 per year, much below the €82 the ANWB was charging. Route Mobiel's proposition to the customer was focused on basic automotive support service with many flexible aspects to suit different customer needs. Customers could build up their contracts in a manner that best suited their personal needs, and they only paid for the elements of choice. At the same time, Route Mobiel set up a business model with little investment, leveraging assets and services of third parties, enabling them to keep prices low. At the time of launch, Route Mobiel employed just ten people.

Route Mobiel's initial offer was far more limited than ANWB's basic package, as they did not offer any services such as magazines, maps, golf memberships, driving lessons and the like. With increased mobile phone penetration, it was not necessary to invest in and maintain a telephone infrastructure as managed by the ANWB. Muller and Schröder primarily targeted customers who were only interested in road-side support, and aimed to eliminate the 'extras' that they believed did not did not add to the basic functionality of road-side assistance. In doing so, a lower-priced service could be offered.

Route Mobiel found a way to outsource the very service it was founded for – road-side support. Different to the ANWB, which owned 1,100 full service cars, Route Mobiel created a commercial relationship with a group of independent garages, combined in one overall organization, Europ Assistance, that could also provide timely road-side assistance. Europ Assistance was initially created to mainly remove defective or damaged cars from the highway, but by the early 2000s had contracts with several car-lease companies to provide roadside repairs. Through its relationship with Europe Assistance, Route Mobiel could access 1,300 car service engineers in 180 locations across the Netherlands without any direct investment in support vehicles or the training of automotive technicans. In cases where a defective car could not be fixed at the roadside, the car would be brought to a garage or to the member's home residence. Route Mobiel only had to pay Europ Assistance for the volumes of service provided, and could therefore adapt its costs to flexibility in sales. In contrast ANWB had permanently employed car service engineers on payroll.

The widespread network of service engineers enabled Route Mobiel's agents to deliver roadside assistance in less than 30 minutes in more than 90% of cases. A test by the consumers Union ("Consumentenbond") showed that Route Mobiel was indeed faster than the ANWB. Route Mobiel's agents reached the place of a car problem in 71% of cases within 30 minutes, compared to 64% for the ANWB. In addition to promising cheaper prices and faster response times, Route Mobiel offered much more flexibility in cancellation and duration of contracts, multiple drivers and coverage ranges, as well as "no claim' reductions and lower rates for second car memberships. This concept was quite new in a market where there was previously a 'one size fits all' approach. Route Mobiel made it possible to get service for only 3 months, and without the obligatory membership fee required by the ANWB. Route Mobiel started with offering flexible contracts (3 months or 12 months). With the ANWB members were obliged to take certain services they might not need, and always for a year.

Route Mobiel offered automotive support services in Europe without the obligation to also acquire automotive support services in the Netherlands. Route Mobiel also introduced automotive services for the summer holiday, as the company recognized that many families in the Netherlands travel abroad (Europe) by car only once a year and therefore should not have to pay for the rest of the year. The price for the months June, July and August was €14.50 and available in 44 countries. In this way Route Mobiel was able to offer a lower price for services that customers valued higher.

Another difference with the ANWB was that automotive services with the ANWB was charged per person, but with Route Mobiel the fee was 'per license plate'. Route Mobiel also offered a no-claim discount if a customer had no car trouble in a year (up to 15%), but in the case of many services in a year costs could be charged to the customer, and the contract could be terminated. Route Mobiel also provided for their new customers a service to provide their cancellation to the ANWB. In 2004 this strategy was discussed in the Dutch House of Commons because ANWB would not accept the cancellations from Route Mobiel. This caused a lot of commotion around the brand in the Dutch Media, which was very welcomed by Route Mobiel. The campaign reached a climax just before 15 November, the expiration date of ANWB's annual memberships.

In 2004–2005, the ANWB lost more than 127,000 members to Route Mobiel, and Route Mobiel was forecasting a target of 250,000 members by the end of 2007, and 500,000 by end 2009. The ANWB CEO G. van Woerkom, declared: "We should definitely worry, also for our employment." While the ANWB was eventually able to stabilize membership losses, this came at the expense of profit margins as the company needed to compete more aggressively on price. In 2006 the CEO announced a new plan to cut costs, streamline the business and improve the financial performance of the ANWB. Some 300 car services engineers lost their job and had to work within a franchise concept, the formal organizational structure with business units was changed, and in 2007 agreement was reached with the labour unions on a new collective employment contract for employees of several business units. But despite these measures, the organization was plunged into financial losses in 2007 and 2008.

Conclusion

The strategy adopted by Hirst, which was initially supported by and largely funded through Saatchi, witnessed the emergence of a new market space where Hirst was the first and only player. Although the traditional art world had not consciously ignored the new market created by Hirst, the industry's focus upon the traditional WHO–WHAT–HOW boundaries of art had created a significant degree of blindness to new opportunities. This was not because artists, curators, dealers and others within the art establishment were unintelligent, but because they had come to take for granted the manner in which their industry functioned, and almost no one questioned these deeply held assumptions. In many ways, Hirst's approach paralleled the innovation approach of Tintoretto more than 450 years before, when the young Venetian also challenged the established boundaries of the art world.

Both Saatchi and Hirst fully understood that success in the late 20th Century artmarket could be defined by uniquely differentiated WHO–WHAT–HOW positioning. Despite Hirst's insults to him after the pair's acrimonious split, Charles Saatchi remained a staunch supporter, labelling Hirst a genius and stating: "General art books dated 2105 will be as brutal about editing the late 20th Century as they are about almost all other centuries. Every artist other than Jackson Pollock, Andy Warhol, Donald Judd and Damien Hirst will be a footnote". The success of Damien Hirst has important implications for practicing managers. Managers within organizations need to recognize that their own experience might make them inattentionally blind to opportunities for creating new market space, and must ask themselves if they are blinkered to new WHO–WHAT–HOW opportunities. What might be interpreted through today's eyes as a dark and distant blur might be viewed in the future as a sharp and enlightened flash of wisdom. The challenge for today's managers is nothing less than removing their organization's innovation cataracts.

Additional Literature

Abell, D. (1980) *Defining the Business: The Starting Point of Strategic Planning*, Englewood Cliffs, NJ: Prentice-Hall Inc.

Hughes, R. (2008) Day of the Dead, *The Guardian*, 13 December 2008.

Kim, C. and Mauborgne, R. (1997) Value Innovation: The Strategic Logic of High Growth, *Harvard Business Review*, January–February: 103–112.

Kim, W.C. and Mauborgne, R. (1999) Creating New Market Space, *Harvard Business Review*, January–February: 83–93.

Markides, C. (1997) Strategic Innovation, *Sloan Management Review*, **38**(3 Spring): 9–23.

Simons, D.J. and Chabris, C.F. (1999) Gorillas in Our Midst: Sustained Inattentional Blindness for Dynamic Events, *Perception*, **28**.

Stacey, D. (2008) Who Forgot to Pay Damien Hirst, *Bad Idea Magazine* (online), 7 November 2008.

Vogel, C. (2008) Bull Market for Hirst in Sotheby's 2-Day Sale, *New York Times*, 16 September 2008.

CHAPTER 4

Beuys
Understanding Creativity – Is Every Manager an Artist?

I have always tried to show why art has to do with life. Only from art can a new concept of economics be formed, in terms of human need, not in the sense of use and consumption, politics and property, but above all in terms of the production of spiritual goods.

—Joseph Beuys

The Doorway to the New

Creativity is a widely used term in the context of strategy, innovation, organizational development and leadership. Often, when analytical methods come to an end, people call for creativity. As managers realize that many strategic questions, leadership issues and complex organizational situations are not manageable in a routine manner with the help of facts, safe structure and tight control, the quest for a different approach starts. The more a situation tends to be new in the sense that managers have not faced this or even a similar situation before, and can therefore not draw upon experience or established routines, the more it calls for a new and creative approach to problem solving. In that sense creativity is seen as almost a prerequisite to respond to new and unexpected situations and also to manage change and renewal.

Creativity is, therefore, a key skill for leaders and organizations in order not only to adapt to rapid changes in the market, but also to proactively shape the context in which the specific industry is embedded. But to truly foster creativity in organizations, we have to recognize two different dimensions, the individual and the collective. At the individual level, the manager or employee needs to be able to understand his or her own creative potential, and to initiate creativity. Collective creativity is determined by the way employees interact in order to find new solutions, to innovate and to solve problems. Both levels are often not only tightly connected but intertwined in the way that one kind of creativity needs the other one to fully harvest its potential.

Just think of a group of talented and bright thinkers in an organization whose ideas are continually killed by a domineering and narrow minded manager. Eventually these creative people would stop producing ideas, or perhaps even leave the company. And the other way around, it would be difficult for a bright manger to realize his or her ideas if he or she is not surrounded by peers and subordinates with open minds.

Academic researchers and practising managers have displayed growing interest in creativity in recent years because creativity has been recognized as one of the primary means through which organizations can maintain competitive advantage in a business environment. Academic and popular literature has framed creativity mostly through three interrelated lenses:

1.   Creativity techniques

2.   Stories about the behaviours of creative people

3.   Descriptions of the creativity process

Whilst these approaches can be useful to help organizations manage creativity, they are limited in helping us to appreciate the inherent creative potential of people. As good as most articles and publications in the three described areas are they tend to restrain themselves to define creativity very much from the outside–in rather than inside–out.

This chapter focuses on the mindset required to unleash individual creativity in organizations, how to support this unleashing of personal creativity through new social process models, and how to sustain collective creativity in a wider organizational context. To develop a deeper understanding of the sources of individual and collective creativity we discuss the career of the artist Joseph Beuys (1921–1986), who dedicated his work to understanding the fundamental parameters of art, the creative process and how people can unfold their very own creative potential. Claiming that "every human is an artist", and through his radical approach to philosophy and interpersonal dynamic of creativity, Beuys became one of the most controversial artists of his time. In this discussion of Beuys' approach to creativity we offer practical insights on boosting creativity for individuals and to foster collective creativity within organizations

The Starting Point

Joseph Beuys was born in Krefeld, Germany, an industrial town in the Lower Rhine region close to the Dutch border, in 1921 as the son of the trader Joseph Jakob Beuys and Johanna Maria Margarete Beuys. From an early age Beuys displayed a keen interest in the natural sciences and had considered a career in medical studies. In 1938 he had his eye opening experience for art, seeing pictures of the German Sculptor Wilhelm Lehmbruck (1881–1919). Lembruck's work is dedicated to figurative sculptures. Some of his figures of his late work emphasize the mental aspect of the human condition. For instance, many of his sculptures present the head as the most prominent and important part, with the physical body often losing significance. It is as Lehmbruck wanted to say, that the act of thinking is the core of human condition. Looking through the lens of Lehmbruck's art work Beuys became not only aware of the principles of sculptural work, art and creativity, but specifically he saw through the work of Lehmbruck what he said later are the general principals of life "Everything (in life) is sculpture". Thoughts and the act of thinking is a sculptural process by itself. The experience with Lehmbruck was the artistic bracket in the life of Beuys. In 1985, 11 days before his death, Beuys was honoured with the prestigious Wilhelm Lehmbruck prize. In his speech, knowing that his death would shortly come, Beuys spoke with the words "to carry on the flame" about his early experience with Lehmbruck.

In 1940 Beuys volunteered for the German Air force. He began his military training as an aircraft radio operator in 1941, but was attending lectures in biology, botany, geography and philosophy during times of leave. Beuys was almost killed, when his aeroplane, a Junkers 87 bomber, crashed in North Africa in 1944. He was rescued by Nomads, a fact which influenced his art approach in the years to come. Beuys used the situation later to link this experience to the sculptural materials for which he became famous including fat and felt.

After the war Beuys met the sculptor Walter Brüx and the painter Hanns Lamers, who encouraged him to become an artist. He enrolled at Kunstakademie Düsseldorf in 1947 and after switching classes, joined the class of Ewald Mataré. Beuys began to read widely, evolving ideas around science, art, literature, philosophy and spirituality. Beuys finished his formal education in 1951, graduating as master student from Mataré's class. It is hard to say when Beuys professional life as an artist began. For a publication of an exhibition in 1964 he rewrote his vita using the title "Joseph Beuys – complete works = curriculum vita". In doing so he declared that for him there was no separation between work, life and art.

Beuys approach to art could be described as a work of research into the sources of creativity. The artist claimed creativity as the "true capital of human beings", Beuys was searching for a kind of art, where basic questions of the human character and its parameters of creativity are central. For the artist creativity is firstly a mental process, which is then a process of shaping material as a conscious act. So it becomes understandable, why he saw ideas, which led to materialization, as material as well. With this broad approach Beuys was able to work as an artist in many fields. He even expanded his work into the political, the economic and the educational spheres by forming social situations as qualified interaction and meaningful structure. For instance Beuys was an early member and one of the founders of the environmental political party The Greens in the late 1970s.

FIGURE 4.1 Joseph Beuys, "Guidelines for a new society", 1977 (Installation made for an interactive talk with visitors)

Right from the beginning of his career, Beuys questioned the traditional understanding of art. Through his production he aimed to enhance an anthropological understanding, where art became an instrument of life-science.

In that sense he saw his artworks as a forum, where people could meet each other in order to talk about the implicit ideas of creativity, the conditions of humanity and social questions. Instead of presenting art as a product to admire, Beuys was aiming more for a dialogue that was provoked through a piece of artwork. He saw dialogue as something that could be shaped, in terms of the quality of interaction in communicational processes in order to make different perspectives become clearer and create common understanding. Beuys saw this process very much the same way as forming a physical sculpture. Dialogue was for

Beuys the social form of a sculpture. Many of his artworks transported this idea and were strategically produced in order to initiate a dialogue. Two examples explain how far he stretched the idea and lived that concept.

Artworks as Ambassadors – Key Works and Materials

In 1974 when Beuys was invited to the exhibition "Art into Society – Society into Art" at the ICA in London he was asked what kind of space or material he would need. Nothing specifically was his answer. All he took with him to the exhibition were a couple of old school blackboards and some tripods. Instead of presenting a ready piece of artwork, he started a dialogue with the visitors of the exhibition about his understanding of art and creativity. Through ongoing lectures Beuys talked about his concept of creativtiy, by which every human being is an artist, general ideas of renewal of society and the fundamental understanding of a different democratic model. During his talks with the visitors Beuys was constantly drawing diagrams and words on the blackboards in order to illustrate his ideas. It was pretty much like a classroom lecture. When one of the blackboards was full, he took it and threw it to the floor. Beuys called it a "Throw Performance" (Wurf Aktion). Through the ongoing dialogue and performance the blackboards started to cover the whole ground of the space after a while. What Beuys literally did, was throw ideas to the ground. In doing so the artist created a compelling image, that the blackboards, covered with ideas and social concepts, were the new foundation, people could step on, start to pick up the ideas and work on their renewal.

The performance, which was called *Richtkräfte für eine neue Gesellschaft* (Deflecting force for a new society) was not finished after the exhibition. In fact Beuys used several opportunities during other exhibitions to work, together with visitors, on that piece. He finished it in 1977 and left the blackboards, tripods and some other materials as an installation. This work is one of the centrepieces of the artist, showing relics of an intensive dialogue.

As we look to the artwork now, we do not know in detail what Beuys was talking about, but some parts of the blackboards with their drawings function as relics to foster our imagination of what might have happened. The key of the artwork is, that without the dialogue the artwork itself wouldn't exist. Beuys used the ideas, which emerged during the dialogue, as "material" for his performances and claimed, that the dialogue itself could be seen as a sculpture, a sculpture which truly exists in the social field.

Beuys used this principle in many of his other works. Another example is the installation called *Honigpumpe* (*Honey Pump*), which he built for the "Documenta" exhibition in Kassel in 1977. This installation was a visualization of the process of developing social awareness and the need of positive – warm energy – in human interaction. It consisted of a motor, which was installed at the ground level of the building, embedded with fat, some containers of honey and a long tube system. That system carried the honey throughout the exhibition building right to the roof, where it ended in so called *Kopf Stück* (*Head Piece*), a U-form shaped copper tube. Beuys used the installation *Honigpumpe* as an image for the human blood circulation system, with the motor as a methaphor for the heart and the head piece for the head. Similar to the blood circulation system, the honey flow quickly reached the motor and came almost to a stop at the head piece.

Reflecting ideas of human conditions and matters of community building, Beuys consequently used the installation *Honigpumpe* in order to talk each day of the "Documenta" (100 days) with visitors about the "true capital of human beings" – creativity, his understanding of a human related concept of art and ideas on how to renew the social and political system. Again in the same way as with the blackboard installation, Beuys declared the dialogue as the real sculpture and the physical artwork as only the vehicle for communication. He explicitly said that the installation itself should not be completed before visitors entered the exhibition space and started to talk about what they saw and what ideas were triggered through perceiving the art work.

His choice of material, like fat, felt, bees wax or honey, often referred to Beuys reflection of the human condition. For example the fat and felt material, which he got to know during his wartime rescue by Nomads, reflected the need of human beings to keep the warmth of the body (felt) and to provide the body with energy (fat). Honey refers to the bee population, which was described by nature orientated scientists as a perfect and effective organizational system, thereby reflecting its value for human community building.

Make the Secrets Productive, Every Human is an Artist

The fundamental ideas of Beuys about creativity are found in his most quoted statement: "every human being is an artist". When he placed this statement into the exclusive art world at the beginning of the 1960s, it initiated a shock. At that time the artist was already well known in the growing art market. The statement had such a provocative potential, that artist colleagues, art dealers and buyers, all players of a new art market which for the first time followed strictly financial directions, were afraid to lose exclusivity. The statement was a challenge to the established view of art: could everyone produce art and could everyone say what art is, if everything is art?

"Every human being is an artist" is not about taking up visual arts or writing (though this may be part of it). Rather, it's about mobilizing everyone's latent creative abilities – engaging one's creative thoughts, words and actions and expressing this creativity in meaningful ways to shape and form wherever it is needed. In this sense the statement becomes a deeper sense if extended to "if you risk the debate with yourself". This means to find out in which area your creativity is mostly developed. Beuys said if you ask yourself who you are and what your very own ability is, everybody could be creative – being an artist in his own field of profession.

Beuys offered through his performances, sculptures and teachings concepts that people could actively work with in order to have better access to their own creative potential. How far he stretched the concept can be seen through the installation *Zeige Deine Wunden* (*Show your Wounds*). The core of the installation consisted of two medical stretchers. The installation could be seen as a modern form of Memento Mori as it points to illness, weakness and the end of life. Beuys saw the installation as a sick room where the observer is confronted with his own mortality. Beuys pointed to the idea that the observer, imaginatively showing his wounds, can work through his past until he achieves healing. The artist often said that a human should work through his mental condition as a good preparation for life. Pretty much like you mill a piece of clay before you start to build a sculpture, he recommended that through inner reflection access to ones very own creative potential could be achieved. During this exploration, so the artist said, you might come to places which were injured during the past, but facing theses injuries, or central issues in a person's life, often bears the highest potential for creativity.

Through his whole body of artwork, Beuys describes three core concepts for the path to creativity. This path starts from the inside, the personal creativity, to the outside, initiating creativity in a social context. The three concepts are:

1.   The active form of thinking – personal creativity

2.   The sculptural theory – process creativity

3.   The social sculpture – collective creativity

Let's turn to each of these three concepts in turn.

1. Personal Creativity – The Active form of Thinking

The first product of human creativity is the thought . . . I like to make this idea visible literally as an object to people and its process of origin. Out of that I say: Thinking is sculpture. The active forms of thinking are Intuition, Inspiration and Imagination. The word image is present in that term. Imagination means the image – imago . . . we have to discuss this that thinking can have such a pictorial power

—Josef Beuys

Most of the thinking we do every day, said Beuys, is a routine. We repeat patterns and come up with solutions we already know. Think about a situation where you are at a traffic light and waiting to cross the road. One does not think what a beautiful light it is; the routine says if it turns to green then walk. For daily orientation it is a very functional and important behaviour.

But what do we do if we want to generate new ideas in order to invent or re-invent processes and products? That's the point where thinking must change. In order to generate new ideas we have to let go of well-known patterns of thinking and old solutions. We have to enter what Beuys describes as the active form of thinking. Thereby he talks about three areas: inspiration, intuition and imagination. How do the three areas interrelate?

Inspiration   Let's start with Inspiration. This could be seen as the very moment where we spot something new or get the first spark of an idea. Sometimes people speak about the refreshing "click" or the "Aha" or "Heureka" experience when a moment like this happens. A common experience is that we get stuck thinking about a problem we have to solve. A useful way to open up for inspiration again is to relax and just look for other things. By adopting that attitude we start to let ideas come to us, instead of pushing too hard. The idea might come in a moment you do not expect and might be a bit blurred, but in order to foster inspiration and open up for real new ideas it is important to tolerate that moment of uncertainty. To sharpen the very first idea too quickly might lead us to fall back to old concepts. We have to "download" or to let go all of these old patterns and solutions first.

People, who are well connected with the flow of this very first moment of ideas, are often seen as the "idea giver" or the visionary in teams. They often have a good access to a "field" of ideas, which they can relate in an associative (not functional) manner to the topic they are thinking about.

The way Beuys constantly renewed his approach towards his work, never using the same visual for an idea again, demonstrated his inspired mind which was capable of constantly re-examining his main artistic topic of human creativity from many different angles.

Intuition   Through intuition we begin to sense what the idea could be and start to develop an emotional side. This second step is what most people can clearly experience in everyday life and is an important part of the creative process. Highly intuitive people tend to sense and feel the quality of an upcoming idea before analysing it too much in detail

Recent research on intuition and decision making demonstrated that participants who tended to make spontaneous decisions were, on average, much more satisfied with their choices than participants who were carefully analytical. We might therefore suggest that intuition makes an idea compelling as it is more closely related to emotional feelings. One broadens the first spark of an idea, which becomes an emotional "body". One "feels" the idea and in that sense might find it more compelling for oneself and others.

If we look at highly successful people and ask them about the secret of their success, we often get the answer that in the process of thinking about a problem they sensed more than they thought about the topic. They might say: "I followed my intuition or instinct". They trusted their gut feeling. CEOs of family businesses are often very capable at intuitive decision making, as they often have a deep emotional tie to the business context in which they are embedded.

Beuys played with this concept of intuition, when he produced the artwork *Intuitionskiste* (*Intuition Box*) in 1968. As an instruction to his audience, Beuys declared that the box should be used as a receptacle and filled with things of daily need, or in a metaphorical way, with new ideas.

Imagination   Imagination is the final step – what comes to us as a first spark of an idea and becomes more real by sensing it through the step of intuition now crystallizes as an image. In the process of creativity we start to let the image grow and make it as concrete and powerful as possible in order to communicate the idea. People in organizations who have a strong ability for imagination are often able to visualize changes. For instance they can look at a process from the end, as if it had already been accomplished. By creating an image they make a complex process visible and in that sense more easily understandable.

Beuys understood the power of creating images for complex concepts very well. He characterized his whole artwork as instruments to talk about the conditions of humanity. In the artwork *Straßenbahnhaltestelle* (*Tram Stop*) from 1976, he displayed the importance of decision making, coming from the past and travelling into the future, by using a heavy tram switch leading in two different directions in the installation.

Implications for Managers and Organizations

The active form of thinking is, according to Beuys, the cornerstone of creativity. It is very much an intrinsic driven process. The challenge with this concept, however, is that most of the time the three steps of inspiration, intuition and imagination develop themselves so quickly that it is difficult to be cognisant of them. Creative people who engage in this form of active thinking are more often than not unaware that they even follow this mental path. Therefore, to think creatively in a purposeful manner needs meta-cognition – the ability to think about ones thinking processes.

The manner in which Beuys stretched the topic of the active form of thinking can be seen by recent brain research. Gerhard Roth of the University of Bremen says: "All decisions are at the end decisions based upon emotions, which are the fundament of our motivation". In a summary article of the *Annual Review of Psychology* in 2006, the brain researcher Elizabeth Phelps of the New York University states: "To understand human thinking, we have to consider the emotions". More and more cognition researchers have started to appreciate a fact that Beuys knew well: who wants to think, must feel first.

Although inspiration, intuition and imagination are tightly connected with each other and it is first of all a concept of personal mastery, companies can work with this concept in order to spark creativity within their workforce/executives.

Inspiration   As the very first moment in the process of creativity, inspiration needs two things that can seem contradictory. It needs a framework, a rough idea of where to go and the open attitude of having no clear objective. The framework, which could be seen as wide side rails, creates the tension. You are aiming for something you don't know exactly in order to get a direction and to go forward. The open attitude means to stop in order to create the space where ideas can be developed and find their place. The stop and go dynamic is essential to foster inspiration, to give ideas a chance to enter the thinking space.

Take the example of Pixar. Pixar produced its first motion picture *Toy Story* in 1995, followed by other films like *Monsters Inc* and *Finding Nemo*. The ongoing

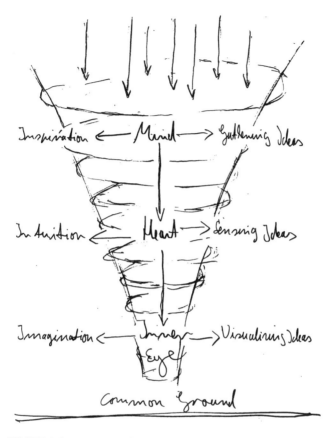

FIGURE 4.2 Drawing of inspiration, intuition, imagination

success of their films is not only a consequence of the increase in the animation technique, to which a movie audience adapts quite quickly. Knowing that their audience wanted to be constantly surprised from one film to the next, Pixar did not over emphasize technical effects despite being expert in technical wizardry. The company understood precisely that they were in the story-telling business and needed, in that sense, in nearly every single scene of a film an unusual and new idea, something which would surprise the viewer again and again. While the plot of Pixar films might not be so complicated, which is also a part of the strong success, the individual scenes are unique in the way in which they are created. Three and a half years before the movie *Finding Nemo* was released the Pixar team started to create the first drafts of the storyboard. Nearly half of the production time was used to work out every tiny element of the story. Each scene is full of little details like the design of characters, colours, light and so on. Pixar understands that it might only be the eye blink of a fish which excites the customer and makes the difference.

In the production teams of Pixar thousands of ideas are constantly being created, even though most of them are never used. This process is ongoing research for the real "new". While animation techniques to create a movie are provided to animators, Pixar gives all its production teams the freedom to explore new ideas within a broad creative framework. The company's management readily admits that most of the ideas at Pixar would not emerge if managers did not allow for uncertainty and openness.

Fostering inspiration in an organization needs first of all managers who have a sense of the dynamic of this particular creative energy, which can be more easily destroyed than built. Further these managers need an understanding of the dramaturgy of exploring ideas. This dramaturgy is mostly about the combination of a guiding general but well chosen question, which is key for the quality of a process to unleash inspiration, and the freedom to let things happen, rather than to control them.

Intuition   Intuition is the emotional side of the active form of thinking. In many organizations it is uncommon to base decisions on intuition as this is seen as irrational and does not fit into the "appropriate way" of dealing with business challenges. Family organizations often have a culture which is more open to that.

Wedelin von Boch, CEO of the ceramic producer Villerory & Boch, stated in an interview that consumer decisions are 85 percent intuitive taken. He claimed this insight, the making of intuitive decisions, is an essential success factor for Villeroy & Boch when placing new product lines in the market. He says the unique value proposition of the company is design, which cannot be judged by rational decisions.

Companies can support intuition actively in the sense that they create a trustful and respectful atmosphere where employees are not forced to rationalize in the majority approved way. Intuition, as the second part of the creative process, needs individuals to have the space to turn a problem upside down in order to be able to explore and evaluate all different solutions. The biggest challenge in fostering intuition, which can be found mostly in big organizations, is that they have a culture based upon too much structured analysis, political manoeuvring and rationality. Instead of thinking and communicating freely about the emotional part of decisions, employees tend to stick to the organization's hierarchy and often try to rationalize their ideas. If you ask people why they didn't contribute their ideas, the answer is often one of the following: "I thought that my boss would not like my idea" or "I had no rational argument to support my idea". Lots of ideas and important insights are easily lost if there is no culture for the emotional side of organizational needs and intuition.

Managers can think about how to approach important decisions differently. They can invite their management team to a meeting to find out what might be the right direction by presenting them different concepts. Instead of asking for clear statements right away by rationally analysing the concepts, the manager can ask their team first to use their intuition and to talk about the concepts by their gut feeling. The manager can invite team members to reflect individually for a moment and then ask them to contribute, to share how they see the different concepts and what they feel. People might say: "It feels good, because it has to do with . . . ", or "I don't like it, as last time when we tried this we ran into a lot of trouble". By allowing people to contribute and deeply share what they sense, the manager can open the space for intuition. This has two effects. By listening to their teams, managers can hear about opportunities and challenges from a different, non-analytical, side. First, teams can appreciate their managers own uncertainty with different solutions and, second, it can bring many different approaches to the issues under consideration. This can help to reassure and adjust the manager's own intuition and might develop a broader picture of the strategic question in order to make a final decision.

Imagination   The last step on the path to improved creativity is imagination, the ability to visualize a desired future estate, which is so powerful that it helps people to overcome potential obstacles.

Think again of Pixar. In order to strengthen the imagination capabilities within Pixar the company changed the mission of their development teams. Instead of coming up with new ideas for movies, as is the role at most studios, their job was to assemble small incubator teams to help directors refine their own ideas into powerful visions/pictures of potential films that were then presented to the management board. Pixar does not judge teams during this incubation stage by the material they produce, but by their imagination and the teams' social dynamics created through this common vision of the future that helps the team to solve problems and make progress.

Imagination might be one of the most important competencies for managers in constantly changing market environments. It is not only imagining when and how the company will have to change, much more it is the need to create meaning through an image which people in the company understand, relate to and are open to following. The process of imagination and the communication of the emerging images are key for an alignment process in an organization.

2. Process Creativity – The Sculptural Theory

A fundamental aspect in Beuys' concept of creativity and a key to the understanding of his artwork is his sculptural theory. The artist believed that every material could be in a state between two poles: the pole of structure and the pole of movement.

Beuys related the pole of movement with activity, warmness, energy, movement, intuitive thinking, but also disorder and chaos. The pole of structure he related to form, coldness, organization, systematic, rational thinking and structure. Beuys believed that everything from thoughts to real material oscillated between these two poles.

Let's see how he used that concept in his artwork. For instance wax and fat, were used for the famous sculpture *Unschlitt/Tallow* (*Wedge*). This sculpture was created for the first exhibition "Sculptural Projects" in Muenster Germany, 1977. The form of the sculpture was a gigantic wedge (10 × 3 × 2 metres) the artist wanted to place it in a super-technical, clean architectural part of a pedestrian underpass. Beuys saw this place as being too structured, almost as a cold place, and wanted to add some material containing a lot of energy and warmth. So he chose the wax and fat combination for the project in order to balance, as he said, the energy level of the place. The curio was that the sculpture was never placed into its allotted spot during the exhibition. The sculpture was produced in a foundry. After the wax and fat mixture was cast into form it took months to cool down and the sculpture was not released from its mould until after the exhibition had closed. Beuys used the situation and underlined his fundamental artistic statement. As Beuys often claimed that there is a need to bring more

FIGURE 4.3 Drawing of the two poles of creativity

warmness (emotional quality) into the thinking process, he produced a glass cabinet containing some of the material and wrote down the sentence: "Beuys produced a sculpture which does not cool down".

In a different example titled *Das Ende des 20. Jahrhunderts* (*The end of the 20th Century*) Beuys worked with basalt stones. He assembled them as a drifting field of stone columns and added a pallet lifting truck. The whole installation looked like a workshop situation. Using that cold and very structured material the artist questioned what might come after a century where humanity emphasized so much on meaning of rationality and structure.

Beuys claimed that this principle was not only relevant for art production. He said it had validity for all processes, also processes in the social context and processes of communication. In his understanding of the expanded concept of art, material could also be what people think, say or contribute to a process.

Process creativity, according to Beuys, is the active shaping of a situation (by adding more structure or chaos), instead of controlling it. In this sense the process itself becomes creative. To manage process creativity the individual has to closely observe the situation and judge upon its tendency towards structure or chaos. Think about a typical situation in an innovation process inside a company where a manager has to deal with complex situations and people's different ideas. Sometimes during the project there might be a tendency to lose focus, the situation becomes too chaotic and unstructured. According to Beuys you now have to add more structure without ending the process. Or the other way around a situation has a tendency to be stuck. The communication is over-structured and the team might run out of ideas. Now it's time to light the fire again and to encourage people to rethink the problem from a different angle or bring in external experts. The overall focus of a manager in this process is not so much the single contribution; it is a good deal more the quality of communication. An alert perception is the key competence in that process.

An organization that has excelled in "sculptural" or process creativity is Ideo, the California based design company. In a widely known project for an ABC television feature a group of about 15 individuals at Ideo was brought together to redesign the supermarket shopping cart. The eclectic group was divided into a number of work teams who came up with hundreds of new ideas. But at a certain moment, the project leader realized that the team would need more structure and said: "This is the moment where we call the adults to the playing field". But instead of telling the project teams what to do the project leader simply narrowed down the potential options by deciding on four key needs areas for the shopping cart: shopping, safety, security and finding what you are looking for. While this structured the process it did not kill creativity because from here the team members were invited to build on the already existing ideas and focus them on the identified need areas. If a project team got stuck the project leader's role was to stop the process and encourage the team to do different things. This opened the situation by bringing in more chaos, more excitement and passion or, in the words of Beuys, more "warm energy".

3. Collective Creativity – The Social Sculpture

When Beuys was asked to name the most important piece of artwork that he ever produced, he always answered that it was the concept of the "Social Sculpture". Claiming a concept to be a "real" piece of art might be an unusual answer. What he did in fact was bring together two different things, social behaviour and the principles of building a sculpture. Consequently, thinking as an artist Beuys saw the interaction of humans as a sculptural space which could be shaped, on a metaphorical level, in the same way as a real sculpture. According to the artist a social sculpture can be "built" by using sculptural thinking, which is the key to the concept of Social Sculpture. "Sculptural Thinking" is the mindset for individuals to perceive things around them. With this idea Beuys stepped beyond the famous concept of Paul Klee, who developed in his time as a Bauhaus teacher in the 1920s the concept of "Bildnerisches Denken" (pictorial thinking).

The differences between "Pictorial Thinking" and "Sculptural Thinking" are fundamental.

Klee describes the perception of a two dimensional artwork, because we can observe a whole painting at once, as a walk with our eyes over the painting in front of us. We don't have to change our perspective. – The perception of a sculpture is totally different. We have to change our point of view as we are obviously not able to see the whole sculpture at once. We have to pick up different viewpoints in order to see the sculpture. As we start our observation by moving around, beginning with one particular view, we gather other views and finally come back to the starting point where again we do see the same thing we did when we started, but obviously not the back side. However, different from the beginning of our observations, we have a memory of what we saw. Based on these memories of different perspectives and information we "construct" the image of the whole sculpture and have now a better ability to form an opinion about the observed object.

Think about a simple piece of paper somebody holds in front of you. You look at the paper from the side and you see more or less a thin fine line. Not before you change the perspective are you able to say what the real dimension of the paper is. Beuys labels this process of assembling the different perspectives as "Sculptural Thinking".

The artist claims that this principle is valid for the social context as well and that we do the very same thing, shaping space, whether we build a real sculpture or work together with people. Think about how you get to know somebody for the first time. You will memorize this experience. Now you see the person again, maybe in a different context and add this new impression to the former one. Each time you see the person you add different experiences and get to know the person better. This is exactly what Beuys claims is a social sculpture. It is the relatedness to another person or belonging to a team, which is built through perception and dialogue.

Certainly the material of the social context is different from traditional materials of a sculpture. But Beuys speaks about thoughts, ideas and emotions as material as well. But, while in the context of the sculpture the object in itself provides the opportunity to be looked at from different angles (perspectives), in the social context the different perspectives are provided by different members of a team that work together to shape an idea and to start, for example, an innovation process.

While different perspectives are key, Beuys also stresses the idea that the quality of the dialogue itself is essential to the outcome of the Social Sculpture. The result, he said, is mainly influenced by the creative tension of the process, which is supported by a broad framework and at the same time an open attitude. Here the open attitude mainly refers to the fact that each member of the team is seen as equal, team members respect each other regardless of their background, and everybody shares the vision that diversity adds value.

Four examples show the fundamental impact of Beuys' concept of Social Sculpture nowadays. Even if in all four examples the organization might not use Beuys' term explicitly, it is possible to identify strategies and concepts that are directly related to the artists innovative thoughts. All of these strategies and concepts share one key element: dialogue as a way to share and integrate different points of view in order to unleash creativity and construct an innovative perspective for the organization.

Ideo: Whenever an innovation process is started in the company the composition of the team is key. As in the case of the shopping cart project the team included a Stanford engineer, a Harvard MBA, a linguist, a marketing expert, a psychologist and a biology major. That setting enables multiple perspectives that are needed and described by Beuys to start a real creative process, But, even more important than the pure diversity is the respect among the team members, their being seen as equal and working towards a shared vision. As hierarchical structure is often present in established companies, innovation teams must be composed with attention to diversity. It must be clear that there is a space where "normal" hierarchies do not apply and people are not blamed for stepping out of the roles of usual hierarchical levels.

Business Schools: In top-tier business schools it is not unusual to find two very different kinds of faculty: the ones that excel in teaching and the others who focus on research. Only if these two types are treated equally by the management of the institution and respect each other as real colleagues, can they create an inspiring and unique atmosphere that fosters practical knowledge transfer. Bringing these two kinds of faculty together by increasing sociability and solidarity of purpose can open a strong stream of practical research to the customer facing side of the business, while at the same time enabling academics to know what kind of impact their theories have through customer feedback. Out of this unique mixture of the two business schools can develop approaches that are relevant to academics and management practitioners alike. But this approach still tends to be the exception rather than the rule.

Industry: Think of a typical engineering driven machine tool company. Here we can often make the interesting observation that the best engineers are working in R&D, while those with the lower educational qualifications start in production. Sales teams are often staffed by engineers who did not make it into R&D or production. In some companies these hierarchical divisions are so engrained into the DNA that when you start to build an eclectic team with participants from R&D, production and sales there is diversity but respect between the members is very hard to establish. This problem is important to acknowledge. In a situation like this managers have to break the rules of hierarchy, for instance by creating a space whereby definition of the rules of interaction and communication of the organization are played differently from the usual approach.

Without a respect for individual skills and expertise, as well as a compelling shared objective, team performance can be far from ideal and conflict can readily emerge. To foster creativity it is therefore essential to refresh the organization's behavioural patterns. This happened when Volkswagen decided to let Audi develop its own line of automobiles in 1994. It was a unique chance for the company and a moment where a cross-functional team was set up in order to create a new brand. The small team felt very much like an elite within the company and established its own rules of collaboration. In 1997 the team launched the Audi TT which helped to propel Audi's image from a family car producer, to a modern sports car manufacturer to compete with brands such as Porsche, BMW and Lexus.

Consultancy: The consultancy company Egon Zehnder, specializing in executive research, recognized in many projects at CEO level that top leaders often have the ability to initiate a culture of dialogue. Further, these top leaders frequently have a strong ability to recognize the various skills and abilities of their employees, and use this as a resource to generate new value. They coordinate the different abilities of people in order to create better alignment with the market or to kick off innovation processes within the company.

Egon Zehnder developed an appraisal format to look at the creative potential of top-level management. According to the firm's experience it defined creativity at the managerial level in the following way:

- A top-level manager with high creative potential should have the understanding and ability to foster constructive dialogue within the organization.

- He or she is highly skilled to initiate such a process by inviting people to share their perspectives.

- A high-performing manager uses these contributions in order to gain a better understanding of complex situations and is able to invest in the various processes of organizational change at an emotional level.

But Egon Zehnder also recognized that a highly talented manager might not even talk about creativity or recognize what he or she is doing as fostering creativity. Rather, the manager has an intrinsic understanding and experience of creativity and creates situations to initiate ongoing renewal within the organization.

Conclusion

By looking at Beuys and understanding his approach towards creativity, managers can become aware of ways to enable people to unfold their very own creative potential. The approach of Beuys provides valuable insights for the manner in which managers can foster individual creativity within their organizations, and also develop processes, structures and an environmental context conducive to collective innovation. Managers need to acknowledge that despite the emergence of analytical, metrics-driven approaches to problem solving, imagination, inspiration and intuition still have a very important part to play in the modern business.

Rather than being constrained by the boundaries of established management culture and legacy organizational practices, managers should recognize the potential to sculpt their organization's innovation practices and social interactions, just as Beuys created new forms of artwork through his understanding of the process of creativity. The interaction of humans within an organization can be seen as a sculptural space, which can be shaped, on a metaphorical level, in the same way as a real sculpture to boost innovation and creativity. Perhaps the term "creativity sculpturing" should become a core part of the management lexicon for the 21st Century.

Additional Literature

Amabile, T.M., Conti, R., Coon, H., Lazenby, J. and Herron, M. (1996) Assessing the work environment for creativity, *Academy of Management Journal*, **39**(5 October): 1154–1184.

Amabile, T. and Khaire, M. (2008) Creativity and the role of the leader, *Harvard Business Review*, October, **10**: 100–109.

Brown, T. (2008) Design Thinking, *Harvard Business Review*, **92**(June): 85–92.

Catmull, E. (2008) How Pixar Fosters Collective Creativity, *Harvard Business Review*, **86**(9 September): 64–72.

Hall, G. (2008) Inside the theory of U, *Reflections*, **9**(1): 41–46.

Harlan, V. (2010) Was ist Kunst? *Urachhaus*, Auflage; 6. A.

Malakate, A., Andriopoulos, C. and Gotsi, M. (2007) Assessing Job Candidates' Creativity: Propositions and Future Research Directions, *Creativity and Innovation Management*, **16**(3 September): 307–316.

Ready, D.A. and Conger, J.A. (2007) Make Your Company a Talent Factory, *Harvard Business Review*, **85**(6 June): 68–77.

Stachelhaus, H. (2006) *Joseph Beuys, Neuausgabe*, List Tb; Auflage.

CHAPTER 5

Picasso, van Gogh & Gauguin
Art Lessons for Global Managers

Introduction

The emergence of globalization in its current form has been seen as both a threat and an opportunity for firms, and has spurred an increasing interest in managing the global paradigm. Globalization has been driven by great advances in technologies, with different waves of technological evolution dramatically reducing the time, costs and complexity of international movement and communication. These technological advances have shrunk the world, and in turn forced sociocultural adaptation and change. In some cases, the evolution of technology that has underpinned globalization has disrupted established industries, and firms that have not been able to adapt have been swallowed or disappeared from the business landscape. Other organizations have recognized the seemingly unrelenting march of globalization as an opportunity for growth, and have used innovation and creativity to break beyond national or regional boundaries to become truly international entities. In this chapter we suggest that today's managers can learn much by stepping back and examining the manner in which artists adapted to the increasing globalization of the arts from the mid 19th Century. We specifically explore the work of three artists: Vincent van Gogh, Paul Gauguin and Pablo Picasso. All three of these artists responded in different ways to the increasing inter-connectedness of the world and we draw upon their responses to globalization to provide lessons for the 21st Century global manager.

Early Drivers of Globalization in the Art World: From the Beginning of the 19th to the 20th Century

The Change of the Social System

The French revolution (1789–1799) was one of the most significant events of modern European history. The end of the feudal absolutistic corporative state and the rise of Enlightenment principles of citizenship and the declaration of the Rights of Man and of the Citizen initiated deep changes in society and formed modern understanding of democracy. Before the French revolution, the church and the aristocracy had been the main sponsors of the arts. This market had been strongly focused upon representative art as portraits, religious and mythological topics, or landscapes for the aristocratic class. But through the change of social revolution, civil society was born. This new society also had a demand for representative art, but with a different taste. The new principals expected a style of artwork appropriate to changing social dynamics, for instance referring to the changing role of equality in society or the importance of the upcoming middle class. Artists had to adapt to this demand, for example by portraying a person's status in civil society or by choosing an appropriate background.

Artists like Jacques-Louis David (1748–1825) adapted to the rapid changes in society from the very beginning of the French Revolution. Starting his career as member of the Royal Academy, painting the last king of France Louis the XVI, he became an active member of the French Revolution as a member of the Jacobin party, and was a close friend to Robespierre (1758–1794). In that position he portrayed members of the new civil society. Ironically he finished his career as the court painter of the first French consul and the later self-crowned emperor Napoleon Bonaparte (1769–1821).

The rising demand of the new civil society in France established a growing art market. Paris emerged as the centre of the art world, especially for painters, in the middle of the 19th Century. Different from Florence in the 15th Century and Rome in the 17th Century, where the focus of art activity underlined the status and power of the city-states, the Paris art market identified with the new prominent customers and their political and social status. The "Paris Salon", established in 1667 by Ludwig 14th, was representative of the art market during the pre-revolutionary period, and only open for members of the Royal Academy. After the revolution the institution opened up for other artists as well, but until the 1860s it was still the main (if not only) market for artists seeking access to the new elite; the Salon was still shaped by the aristocratic inheritance of the pre-revolutionary time. While a new "customer" group emerged, these new customers were largely drawn from the elite of the new social fabric of the time.

For many years, accreditation to the Salon exhibition remained the basic requirement to establish a successful art career in France. The selection criteria for works exhibited at the Salon were very conventional, and new ideas were frequently suppressed. The salon displayed mainly the established artists and the number of rejections grew constantly in the 1850s and 1860s. Artists who were excluded from the Salon found it extremely difficult to find customers for their artworks. A prominent example was Édouard Manet's (1832–1883) painting *The Luncheon on the Grass*, which was presented to the Salon jury in 1863. Obviously a very erotic paining, it was officially rejected because of a lack of sense of beauty and technical ability. Today, it is acknowledged as one of the most important paintings of Manet and a key artwork of the epoch.

Manet's rejection made it obvious that even the most talented artists would be rejected by the Paris Salon unless they were willing to conform to the conventional criteria of the institution. This resulted in 1863 in the founding of the

"Salon of the Dismissed" by Napoleon III, which quickly became popular amongst the growing middle classes of Paris society. Famous artists like Claude Monet (1840–1926), Alfred Sisley (1839–1899), Manet, August Renoir (1841–1919) and Gustave Corbet (1819–1877) showed their work at this new salon, and following its success other competing exhibitions were established. In the following years these exhibitions became more and more important and were widely covered by the press. Finally this development resulted in the "Salon of the Independents", which was founded as a "democratic" art space in 1884, and true revolution finally came to the art establishment.

This new emerging market segment became especially interesting for customers who wanted to underline their social mobility and modernity. The artists who exhibited at the Salon of the Independents distinguished themselves from the traditional market represented by the Paris Salon by being innovative and embracing new artistic techniques like pointillism or plein air painting. This tension between the established and the new and upcoming artists drew a lot of attention to Paris and created the so-called "art-spirit of Paris" which persisted until the 1920s and 1930s, attracting famous collectors like Alfred Barnes (1872–1952), who showed his collection of these artists like Manet, Vincent van Gogh (1853–1890), Paul Gauguin (1848–1903), Pablo Picasso (1881–1073) and others in 1923 at the Pennsylvania Academy of Fine Arts.

At the same time that hierarchies and tradition were being disrupted in France, artists were actively looking for inspirations from science, technology and foreign cultures in order to develop new artistic styles and techniques. With the gradual decline of the influence of the Paris Salon, artists were emboldened to look beyond national borders and strict "criteria" that defined what was acceptable as art. Over the period 1850–1900 there were four significant drivers which underpinned this leap in innovation and creativity: the invention of photography, new ways of travelling, the influence of foreign cultures and scientific advances in chemical colourings, optical effects and perception.

Driver 1: Photography as Disruptive Innovation In 1826 Joseph Nicéphore Nièpce invented photography. His technical research to produce a "true life" image began in 1816 when he was successful in transposing a temporary image on a chlorine coated silver paper on his camera *obscura*. After many more and elaborate experiments Nièpce created the first real photograph – a view out of his studio – in 1826. It took him 8 hours to shoot the photo using a special kind of asphalt varnish. In 1835 William Fox Talbot invented the positive–negative procedure and in 1883 the first rasterized photo, an invention of Georg Meisenbach, was printed in the Leipziger newspaper *Illustrierte Zeitung*.

From then on it was possible to reproduce pictures on a larger scale, to deliver them faster than hand-painted artworks, and to produce them at a lower cost. This meant that demand for what had been a significant part of the art production market – the painting of representative and realistic images of people – declined dramatically. Some artists tried to respond to this innovation by developing new painting techniques, for example the well-known portrait painter Franz von Lenbach (1836–1904) who developed a quick painting process (concentrating on only important parts of the picture, leaving the background quite rudimentary) to accelerate production speed and reduce cost. Although von Lenbach had a strong reputation and was highly demanded amongst the civil society (he painted Otto von Bismarck) he recognized the new technology as a competing business. Therefore, Lenbach and other painters imitated various aspects of photography, like the specific short time expression of the portrayed person, which let them look very present and fresh. But these efforts were not able to significantly slow down the decline of the portrait painting industry and artists were forced to discover new artistic forms and expressions that did not compete directly with photography.

At the same time as portrait photography was exploding as a new business in the Western world, it was being used on expeditions to the conquered "new" colonies in Africa and parts of Asia-Pacific. Photography enabled the production of a different quality and quantity of visual impressions of foreign cultures that flooded into the newspapers, periodicals and other publications of Europe. The decline of the market for representative artwork (especially illustrations of landscapes, family situations and portraits) had forced artists to look for inspiration, and ironically for many artists this inspiration was provided by the windows that photography opened to the new world. Simultaneously, the breakdown of the hierarchy and tradition of the Paris Salon and the rise of non-traditional art exhibitions provided new outlets for experimentation.

Driver 2: Easier Ways of Travelling   After more than four centuries of expeditions launched from various countries, like Spain (Christopher Columbus 15th Century, Ferdinand de Magellan 16th Century) or England (James Cook 18th Century), the world was widely explored from a European perspective. With the beginning of the 19th Century came a demand to exploit the colonized countries on a different level and, through this exploitation, to increase the economic power of the colonizers. International travel became much easier from the mid-19th Century and while many European countries, like France, England and the Netherlands, had long established maritime trade routes to the new colonies, the late 19th Century saw an increase of commercial shipping which established cargo and passenger routes on a routine basis. This development was possible mainly through the technical invention of steamboats. For example, the German

Entrepreneur Adolph Woerman (1847–1911) founded a shipping company in 1880 with one steam ship and 12 sailing boats. But the demand for faster travel was so great that he eventually converted his entire fleet to steam power. He was able to offer comfortable trips to South and West Africa that would previously have been expensive, dangerous and beyond the reach of any but the wealthiest members of society.

Beside the trade in commercial goods and commodities such as palm oil, coffee, cocoa and spices, there was also a flow of travelogues, cultural objects, clothes, pottery and jewellery along the shipping routes to Europe. Artists were attracted to cultural objects and the writings of adventurers and explorers, intuitively recognizing the potential therein for their own artistic explorations. Books written by travellers and authors such as Pierre Loti (1850–1923: *Le Mariage de Loti* 1880) created a great deal of interest in the exotic and natural world of the South Seas. *Le Mariage de Loti* (*The marriage of Loti*) was a bestselling book in France for many years, and inspired belief in the idea of a pure and simple life.

It had not been unusual over the centuries for European artists to travel or to study in other parts of the European landmass. But, while artists like Albrecht Dürer (1471–1528) travelled to Italy to learn about new painting techniques, the artists of the late 19th Century increasingly sought different artistic "environments" in which to develop their artistic style. As an example, Vincent van Gogh lived for extended periods in the south of France in order to study the bright and colourful light. Now, as travelling became more affordable, artists began to travel even more widely to seek out creative inspiration and explore intensively how they could integrate exotic foreign influences into their own artistic work.

Driver 3: Discovery of and Influence by Foreign Cultures   With the expansion of colonization a completely new world opened up and Europe was heavily impressed by foreign cultures. This could be seen, for example, in the "World's Fair" initiated in London for the first time in 1851. The goal of such exhibitions was to showcase the uniqueness and characteristics of the colonies under one roof and to present the economic potential of expanding overseas possessions. These exhibitions were European statements about the capability to govern foreign countries, and further more to establish powerful European states as true global empires. But the discovery of the New World and the establishment of the colonies was dominated by a European mindset that was obsessed with exploitation rather than understanding of foreign cultures.

From the 1600s there were three main ways in which Europe perceived foreign lands and their inhabitants. All three perspectives were in place and were discussed with varying emphasis during different times. At the beginning of the great expeditions, around the 15th Century, the foreigner was seen as an equal being. Through the influence of the Dominican monk Bartolomé de Las Casas (1484–1566) who joined Christopher Columbus (1451–1506) on his second journey to the new world, Columbus developed a view of foreigners as equal beings. Las Casas became well known as an early representative for human rights through his dedication to fight for the Indians his expedition met. He saw the discovered inhabitants as potential Christians and subjects of the Spanish crown, and in that way endowed with the same rights.

Later, during the 16th Century, in the time of Hernán Cortés (1485–1547), foreigners were seen as dangerous outsiders that were threatening to "civilized" society. There was debate in Spain about the humanness of the inhabitants of the conquered world and whether they could be colonized or enslaved. These views resulted in atrocities and widespread suffering for the indigenous populations of many colonized countries over a period stretching several centuries.

From the early 1800s ideas of the philosopher and educator Jean-Jacques Rousseau (1712–1778) renewed debate about the status of indigenous people. Rousseau looked at indigenous people as the "other better being" or, as Rousseau said, "the true self outside of us". But the propagation of the ideas of Charles Darwin on the evolution of species also contributed to this debate, with many "educated" Europeans arguing that the subjugation of native peoples was a process of the "natural" selection of more highly developed humans over the less developed.

All three perspectives of the foreigner were projections of Euro-centric thought, and gave little regard to the specific reality of foreign societies and people. So it is little wonder that by the end of the 19th Century opinions sometimes existed as contradiction; debate was not motivated by the necessity to understand foreign cultures. Discussion was often driven by the idea that the inhabitants of the new colonies were not yet in the same developed status as Europeans, and that these foreign cultures would have to follow steps of development to reach the same level as Europe. Ethnological museums with collections of foreign art and artefacts that opened in European cities like Brussels, London, Paris, Vienna and Berlin did little more than present quaint aspects of foreign cultures; Europe was not driven to gain a deeper level of cross-cultural understanding.

Despite the narrow views of foreign cultures at this time, artists gained access to ethnographic collections and were attracted by the flood of foreign objects. Most interesting for artists were the different esthetical attributes of artistic production, like forms, colours, structural elements and composition. Very often they had an artistic approach towards these foreign objects, which meant that they were more interested in simply perceiving the objects for their colours, forms and so on, than understanding cultural background or function. This approach kept the mind open and enabled the artists to mix different creative stimuli on an abstract aesthetic level. They started to play with these experiences, and integrated the foreign into their own artistic approaches in order to develop new styles and pieces of artwork. This experimentation became the attitude and philosophy of the upcoming *avant-garde*.

Driver 4: Scientific Advances on Colour, Optical Effects and Abstract Perception   During the 19th Century, scientist-writers such as Michel Eugène Chevreul, Ogden Rood and David Sutter wrote treatises on colour, optical effects and perception. They were able to translate the scientific research of Hermann von Helmholtz (1821–1894) and Isaac Newton (1643–1727) into a written form that was understandable by non-scientists. Chevreul (1786–1889) was perhaps the most important influence on artists at the time; his great contribution was producing the colour wheel of primary and intermediary hues.

Being attracted to science, the Impressionists were especially interested in the interaction of colour. Artists like Claude Monet did not paint what was apparently real; but instead painted what was perceived in observations of nature. Consequently, the front of a building or the appearance of a landscape could be totally different depending on the light situation. George Seurat (1859–1891) invented Pointillism, a painting style that was strictly based on scientific research of optical effects of colours. Seurat believed that a painter could use colour to create harmony and emotion in art in the same way that a musician uses counterpoint and variation to create harmony in music. Seurat theorized that the scientific application of colour was like any other natural law, and he was driven to prove this conjecture. He thought that the knowledge of perception and optical laws could be used to create a new language of art based on its own set of heuristics and he set out to show this language using lines, colour intensity and colour scheme. Seurat called this language Chromoluminarism. Referring to scientific research, these artists put themselves in the forefront of art development and created an early understanding of what later became the brand of modernity, being the creative class or the *avant-garde* of society.

Another fundamental change was the use of abstract forms in compositions. Paul Cézanne (1839–1906) was the pathfinder for this new approach. He studied landscape and saw in the real situation another reality – the reality of abstract forms. He developed a kind of meditative way to look at landscapes, avoiding the normal perception to focus upon a far away viewpoint, and discovered through that approach the basic geometrical forms like cubes, cylinders and cones behind the nature he observed. Cézanne spoke often about how "not to paint reality", and described painting as a process of "realization". He always aspired to paint what he perceived and not what he could see as real. His lifelong research on what he called "the reality of images" was a fundamental influence upon 20th Century art as it provided the foundations for the abstract movement. His concept influenced many artists like George Braque (1882–1963) and Pablo Picasso. These artists invented, from Cezanne's approach, the idea of Cubism, a radical new artistic concept that integrated different perspectives of an observed object as two dimensional. Through the Cubist approach their own parameters of production of artwork changed fundamentally. For these artists it was no longer important to work with the attitude of perfect realism. They realized Cézanne's artistic concept in material creation.

While the adoption of abstract elements was a break from tradition, artists saw the use of abstract elements as free of the ballast and prejudices that they believed inhibited traditional forms of art production. This method of perceiving without prejudice, and the consequent and purposeful playing with these artistic elements opened up the many different influences that were driving globalization in the mid 19th Century.

Adoption, Integration and Fusion – How Artists Adapted to a Globalizing Art World

Artists had traditionally been experts in dealing with influences in order to make them part of their own artistic language. From the early 16th Century curious objects were integrated, for example in still life paintings, in order to raise the attraction of artwork. For instance the Italian artist Pietro Longhi (1702–1785) painted *Exhibition of the Rhino* in 1751, showing an excited crowd looking at a strange and foreign animal – an African rhinoceros. But this kind of experimentation accelerated towards the end of the 19th Century as artists actively sought to broaden their approaches through influences, innovations, concepts and artistic inventions from foreign cultures.

We see mainly three different ways in which artists dealt with the challenges of globalization in the mid 19th Century: adoption, integration and fusion. Artists' learning from foreign culture through copying artistic techniques, concepts or approaches, for example Vincent van Gogh's experimentation with Japanese woodcuts, was termed *adoption. Integration* was the approach artists such as Paul Gauguin, who brought together his life experience of the South Sea world of Tahiti, with its light and colours, and a classical European understanding of composition, adopted. Finally we will look at Picasso and how he created art works from different European and African influences through the act of *fusion* a completely new artistic approach. We will describe fusion as a strategy that melted different cultural characteristics, in the absence of ethnocentric bias or cultural ranking, to create a new global style.

Adoption: Vincent van Gogh 1853–1890

Vincent van Gogh was born in Zundert, the Netherlands, as the son of a book-maker's daughter and a priest. After leaving school he started his artistic education at the Den Haag department of the art dealer Goupil & Cie. He finished his apprenticeship at the London branch in 1874, which gave him an opportunity to visit the city's thriving museum and exhibition spaces. In 1875 he moved to Paris, where he began to separate himself more and more from social interactions. Over the next three and a half years he tried to succeed in different professions, trying his hand as assistant teacher and later as an assistant priest. He worked as a member of the clergy in the Belgian mines until 1880 when the church declined to extend his work contract. At this juncture in his life he decided to become a painter, and was supported in this transition by his brother Theo who had become an established art dealer in Paris. Theo supported Vincent financially for the remainder of his life, on the basis that he kept the majority of his painting for his financial support. In 1886 Vincent van Gogh moved to Paris to live with Theo and, through Theo's gallery, gained his first access to imported Japanese woodcuts. From 1853 when Japan began to open up to the Western world, these spectacular and unusual artworks reached Europe. In 1887 Vincent van Gogh started to change his style of composition and use of colours under the Japanese influence. In a letter to his brother Theo he wrote on 24 September 1888: "I envy the Japanese for the enormous clarity that pervades their work. It is never dull and never seems to have been made in haste. Their work is as simple as breathing and they draw a figure with a few well-chosen lines with the same ease, as effortless as buttoning up one's waistcoat".

Three of his oil paintings from this period copied Japanese woodcuts of the well-known Japanese artist Hiroshige (1797–1858). Two were perfect reproductions. One was Hiroshige's *Japanese Apricot Garden* from 1857, which van Gogh retitled *Flowering Plum Tree* in his copy of 1887. The other was *Thunderstorm at Ohashi* (1857), which became *Bridge in the Rain* (1887).

It was the influence of Japanese artwork that enabled van Gogh to develop the adventurous painting style for which he would become famous. In other letters to Theo at this time he mentioned the specific Japanese characteristics that he adopted for his work: "the lack of body- and cast shadows, flat area of colours with no alteration – encircled with thin black lines, unusual perspective, tiny displaced figures in a landscape".

Beside the direct adoption of composition styles and colours of Hiroshige's work, van Gogh's choice of motifs was widely influenced by Japanese artworks. This could be seen in the series of blooming fruit trees he painted in 1888. Without the influence of Japanese artworks, and van Gogh's willingness to experiment with this style, the artist's outstanding body of work would never have been conceived.

Japanese artworks influenced many artists in the second half of the 19th Century. In fact "Japonisme" was a widespread phenomenon amongst many European artists like Edgar Degas, Edouard Manet, Claude Monet, Henri Toulouse-Lautrec and others. The interesting point is that all of these artists simply adopted and played with the Japanese aesthetic phenomenon – they were not looking for a deeper understanding of the roots and the mindset of the Japanese culture.

Integration: Paul Gauguin 1848–1903

Paul Gauguin was born in Paris to a liberal journalist father and writer mother. In order to escape the difficult circumstances of the February Revolution in France in 1848, his parents moved with him to Peru. In 1853 the family returned to France, and at the age of seventeen Gauguin joined the French navy, a career that enabled him to travel to South America and to the Polar Circle. In 1872, through the help of his guardian Gustave Arosa, he got a position in a bank where he became wealthy as a stock market dealer. He was able to live a luxurious lifestyle, and fathered five children with his wife Mette-Sophie Gad. As Gustave Arosa was an art lover, Gauguin was introduced to the artworks of Eugène Delacroix (1798–1863), Gustave Courbet (1819–1877) and Camille Corot (1796–1875) among others. Inspired by these artists, Gauguin started to paint in 1876. He was invited to an exhibition of the Impressionists and became a student of Camille Pissaro (1830–1903), the teacher of Paul Cézanne (1839–1906), in 1879. After the crash of the Paris stock market in 1882, during which he lost his job as a banker, he decided to make a living based on his artwork.

Influenced by the literature of Pierre Loti and the writer's incredible success, Gauguin dreamt of a carefree life, free of all boundaries in the South Seas. His vision of life in the Pacific islands was a typical European projection at the time, imagining an ideal, exotic and erotic world – a projection of the noble savage as a counter model to the European civilization. In his talks with his artist friend van Gogh, with whom he shared a studio in Arles in the south of France in 1888, Gauguin often spoke about his dream of the "tropical studio" with the condition of a free and easy life. But Gauguin saw that his friend van Gogh would never leave France and, hence, planned to leave for the South Seas to explore new influences for his artwork. He wanted to come back with plenty of artistic materials, like sketches, in order to create new, never seen artworks. However, Gauguin didn't want just to re-invent art; in fact he was aiming to develop designs for life by presenting these concepts through his artwork. Gauguin was, therefore, one of the first artists who wanted to portray an interconnectedness between life and work. He created the modern myth of the artist as the coherent human, a myth which later became the standard of the artists' *avant-garde*.

Beyond his ideas about life and art production, Gauguin was very aware that his market was not in the South Seas – it was still back in France. So, thinking about how to create a new kind of artwork out of new impressions and ideas, he followed a clear business strategy: "The market needs a different kind of art . . . you have to offer absolutely new motives to the dull customers". Tahiti seemed the place to go to in order to bring together these different aspects of art production and life.

In 1891 Gauguin travelled to Tahiti and was deeply disappointed. What he found was not even close to his projections – through the progress of French colonization and the spread of Christianity the South Sea paradise described by Loti had been lost. His first residence lasted for two years, until 1893 when Gauguin went back to Paris in order to sell the paintings he had produced during those years. But the Paris art public refused the paintings and critics made jokes about his "primitive" artistic style, with Gauguin subsequently becoming very frustrated when he did not receive the financial success and reputation he had expected. When he went back for his second residence in Tahiti from 1895 until his death, he continued painting the lost paradise, very consciously overlooking the things that wouldn't fit into his vision of an ideal world. In his paintings he showed idealistic motives like in the painting *Admirable Land*, reflecting the European projection of "carefree paradise", or he integrated classical European art topics like in the painting *The son of God*.

When Gauguin came to Tahiti he had already evolved a very elaborate painting approach. Even if Gauguin aimed at producing a new style of art, which was free from Euro-centred standards, he followed exactly the trace of the

European projection of the noble other world. As he was deeply rooted in the European understanding of composition and use of colour, he didn't change these elements too significantly from a technical point of view. But what he did during his stay in the South Seas was to integrate his experiences of the different light, colour and forms in a new *form* of artwork. Compared to his European style with muted colours, the artworks of the South Seas were mainly based upon the use of pure, unmixed colours and displayed parts of nature as an interaction of free flowing forms. And he went as far as using French and original Tahitian language titles.

We saw in the two cases of van Gogh and Gauguin that adoption by copying foreign art and integration by melting foreign influences into an existing art approach were two different approaches to dealing with foreign cultures in an increasingly global world. The first concept of van Gogh, ironically developed and improved over many centuries in the Eastern world, was a strict and effective learning strategy. The second concept used by Gauguin was that of an advanced production strategy integrating the new into an existing artistic approach. Both concepts were based on influence, which meant that the original, European-rooted approach was not left behind very much. In the next section we will discuss how Pablo Picasso radically changed his concept of art under the effects of globalization and how he moved forward to fusion.

Fusion: Pablo Picasso 1881–1873

Pablo Picasso was born in the city of Málaga in Spain 1881. He was the first child of Don José Ruiz y Blasco (1838–1913) and María Picasso y López. Picasso's father was a painter who specialized in naturalistic drawings of birds and other animals. Picasso showed an early passion and a skill for drawing, and from the age of seven received formal artistic training from his father in figure drawing and oil painting. Ruiz was a traditional, academic artist and instructor, and in 1891 became a professor at the School of Fine Arts of La Coruña. Observing the precision of his son's evolving artistic technique, Ruiz saw the incredible potential of the teenaged Picasso. He convinced the officials at the Barcelona academy to allow his son to sit an entrance exam for the advanced class at the age of just 13. For this exam students typically needed a month to prepare a portfolio of work, but, Picasso completed the work within a week and the jury of the academy allowed him to enter the school.

A few years later, in 1897, Picasso's father and uncle decided to send the young artist to Madrid's Royal Academy of San Fernando, the country's best art school.

Through this educational experience the young Picasso had the opportunity to get to know the famous Spanish paintings at the Prado in Madrid from artists such as El Greco (1541–1614), Diego Velázquez (1599–1660), Francisco Zurbarán (1598–1664) and Francisco Goya (1746–1828). From these experiences Picasso received not only artistic technical knowledge, like composition and the use of colour, but also a deep appreciation for art history. However, it was not until Picasso stepped beyond the national borders of Spain that his artistic inspiration truly became international.

Picasso arrived in Paris 1901 and saw important artworks by the likes of Paul Cézanne, Edgar Degas (1834–1917) and Toulouse-Lautrec (1864–1901). At this time France understood itself as a country with full colonial power: a network of trading routes was developed, the economy was booming and France was seen as one of the leading countries regarding culture. Big collections, such as that in the Musée d'Ethnographie du Trocadéro, which was founded in 1878, reflected this status. Around this time the foundation for what we now call modern art was established. Many inventions like the exploration of colour effects, the autonomy of abstract forms and the deconstruction of the three dimensional space were already made. Going one step further, modern art, the so-called *avant-garde* raised invention as the key principle. This meant that artists had to constantly re-invent everything they saw. This was distinctively different from former periods where referring to older, established, "original" artists and artwork was part of the artistic approach. Artists started to combine and mix old concepts with a personal perspective, in order to create artworks, which appeared in the art market as new products. This highly competitive behaviour was a typical *avant-garde* attitude. The artists started to play with this dilemma. Sometimes they denied the source; sometimes they referred quite obviously to it.

The experience of living in Paris had a great impact on the young Picasso. Together with his artist colleague George Braque (1888–1963) he developed the famous cubistic style. With their new idea of fragmentation of space and multi-perspectives, which referred to Cézannes idea of the geometrical structure of space, they laid the final cornerstone of the development of modern art. From there on artworks did not represent what was visible and real, but became a reality in themselves and art production became autonomous.

In 1907 Picasso painted *Les Demoiselle d'Avignon*. This key work showed clearly how Picasso had moved forward from *integration* to *fusion,* merging radically different cultural approaches in one piece of artwork. On the one hand in *Les Demoiselle d'Avignon* it is very obvious that Picasso is referring to the painting *Women Taking a Bath*, painted by Paul Cezanne 1885–1887. Picasso referred to this painting in many aspects, for example by using a similar proportion of the painting, almost the same composition and the same number of figures. But the shape of the figures and the "broken background" was painted according to his concept of cubism. Picasso therefore used already existing material and integrated this into his own concept in order to create a new style of artwork.

But Picasso also fused elements into this painting which obviously did not draw on the Cezanne painting. Picasso painted the two figures on the right-hand side differently to the rest of the figures. The heads did not quite fit with the bodies and one head, the right one at the top, had a black background, the other below showed a geometrical form under the chin which differed from the other aspects in the painting. Recent research has revealed that Picasso used specific West African masks as part of this painting, a fact which Picasso kept as an artistic secret.

What Picasso did in this painting was much more than taking the influences of foreign culture and integrating them into established European tradition, as Gauguin did. His approach went much further, combining radically different cultural traditions, which did not really relate to each other, and fusing them into a new concept. His attitude was not to judge which part might be more important. Using different global artistic resources Picasso played, recombined and experimented with what fitted best. Whatever seemed to be appropriate for him as a good solution of composition and a new form of artwork, attracting potential buyers, was the right choice.

For the first time in art history an artist left his own cultural roots in terms of organizing his own and foreign cultural styles side by side. Picasso neither raised the foreign culture as "the better one", as Gauguin did, nor did he subordinate it. In fact he took his own and the foreign culture, despite the fact that he had never been to Africa, as equal experience, in order to create new products. In many of his artworks the African impact is clear to see and sometimes so powerful that the question is: is it a Picasso or something different? Picasso followed this concept of *fusion* all his life, and through this approach his art production became truly global.

The example of Picasso showed the dilemma, but also the enormous potential, which the concept of fusion created. In the process of fusion the artist played with his own cultural identity. Sometimes it seemed as if he would lose his identity. After all in the concept of artistic fusion identity emerged out of the recombination of different cultural elements from around the world. The concept of fusion might also be described as a systematic process of renewal through integrating evolving global trends.

Conclusion

The behaviours demonstrated by European artists in the 19th and early 20th Centuries in adapting to globalization provide valuable insights for the 21st Century global business manager. Indeed, in our work with executives from around the world, both in the developed world and in the developing markets of Asia and Africa, we have witnessed the manner in which the approaches of adoption, integration and fusion are being practised.

Adoption is a necessity for global managers that are facing intensified international competition, and the ability to adopt best practices in areas such as production, quality control and supply chain management that have evolved in foreign markets has become a necessity in many industries. Witness Japanese concepts such as *kaizan (*continuous improvement*)* that have been adopted by firms and industries around the world – first in the developed world, but increasingly in the BRIC economies and other emerging markets.

What few managers know is that the early principles of statistical quality control (SQC) underpinning *kaizan* were developed in the US to improve manufacturing efficiency during World War II. But it was managers such as Kaoru Ishikawa of the Japanese Union of Scientists and Engineers (JUSE) who saw the potential of these practices in resource starved post-war Japan. JUSE imported noted American quality experts such as W. Edward Deming to transfer American best practices and within ten years JUSE had trained nearly 20,000 engineers in SQC methods. This adoption of SQC underpinned the global growth of Japanese firms in subsequent decades, and by the mid-1980s JUSE had registered over 250,000 quality circles with close to two million participants in its activities.

Ironically, while the process of adoption provided a powerful boost to the competitiveness of Japanese firms, the booming US domestic economy saw SQC shelved by many American firms until the 1980s when they were *re-imported* from Japan – the *adoption* cycle had gone full-circle as American managers such as Motorola's Bill Smith recognized the need to *adopt* global best practices. In turn, this witnessed the birth of Motorola's fabled Six Sigma business process in

1986 that today enjoys wide-spread application in many sectors of industry around the world.

Just as Vincent van Gogh had borrowed Japanese technical techniques, the adoption of what had become core Japanese management philosophies has been at the heart of the revival of the American quality movement over the past two decades. And the adoption of international best practices which are continuously evolving in industry after industry will remain an important success factor for the 21st Century global manager.

Another skill of the global manager is to recognize the potential of international best practices and then to *adapt* or *connect* new approaches to fit with the *existing* business reality. This is the process of *integration*, and is currently underway in many industries. The rise of India as a software development and services hub, or the Philippines as a low-cost centre for tax, finance and accounting, has forced global managers to rethink long-established value chain activities to *integrate* business functions across international borders and time zones. This process has not been without its challenges, but global managers now see the integration of extended international value chains as simply the way of doing business in the 21st Century paradigm. Indicative of many in its industry, global financial services provider Deutsche Bank has a seven day a week, 24 hour a day, real-time business system that spans the globe; from New York to London, Bangalore to Manila, Frankfurt to Sydney. Managers such as Lydia Kuratzki, a senior manager with the Bank's Group Technology and Operations (GTO) area, lead people and processes that span the globe. A modern day Gauguin, Kuratzki is constantly pursuing new ways to optimize the use of foreign subsidiaries and international vendors to improve the efficiency and effectiveness of Deutsche Bank's local operations. A software team to develop a new application for Deutsche Bank's retail banking business in Germany is just as likely to be comprised of software engineers from India and Poland as it is from Frankfurt or London.

For the true global manager, the future of competitive advantage comes from the process of *fusion* whereby established business structures, processes and mindsets are left behind to create new business systems that leverage on worldwide learning. Lars Stork, Danish COO of mobile network operator Zain Nigeria leveraged the concept of fusion to great success in growing mobile penetration in the rural regions of one of the African continent's most challenging operating environments. With more than 30 years of international experience that has stretched the globe, Stork's approach exemplifies the *avant-garde* of global management thinking.

Utilizing mobile network technologies and core infrastructure created in the developed world, Stork studied the approaches to distribution and marketing to the rural poor by network operator in India and other parts of Asia before embarking on a detailed exploration of the market and socio-cultural environment in the Nigerian countryside. Through the fusion of modern technology, adaptation of best practices from other developing markets and a deep understanding of the local operating situation he and his management team *invented* a highly innovative operating model and route to market strategy to serve low-income rural customers in Nigeria.

At the heart of Stork's new approach was the Rural Acquisition Initiative (RAI), a micro-franchising model that involved partnerships with local tribes and village entrepreneurs to take shared ownership of Zain's mobile towers, ensuring local marketing and distribution reach and greatly reducing security and maintenance costs. But to create the RAI Stork and his management team had to *unlearn* what they knew about running a mobile telecommunications business in developed markets and fuse together international and local technological, commercial and cultural practices into a new operating model. The success of the RAI has been recognized with a *Global Telecommunications Business* award, and Zain is now leveraging Stork's unique business system into other African markets.

Another good example for the merits of fusion is the way some modern and successful companies organize their globally distributed R&D sites. In the past the reason for local R&D let's say in China for a European company was often purely the adaption of knowledge, design and technology which was centrally developed at the home base to the local market. We can see a major shift in that approach lately. More and more companies are developing deep R&D knowledge in local markets and the information and technology flow is no longer a one-way street but has in fact in some cases even shifted towards more and more know-how and technology flowing from the local markets to the home-base. The reasons for this are multidimensional. There is, for example, the advantage of increasing resource flexibility, the closeness to the customers, the accessibility of functional expertise in the local markets, the potential cost savings on labour and operating costs and last but not least the promise of being able to develop 24 hours, seven days a week. But research has shown that most of the potential merits of globally distributed R&D sites only come into full bloom when management takes "fusion" seriously: in the way that managers from different R&D sites treat each other with respect, that cultural differences are seen as sources of potential competitive advantage not something that is slowing the company down, and that the flow not only of information but also of ideas and people is a two way street with a lot of decentralized decision making and implementing. In that sense companies are able to benefit from differences much more. This is seen as the biggest challenge in times where global players such as Siemens, GE, Bosch or Philips are creating globally dispersed R&D sites where the role of foreign R&D sites is lately changing from merely adapting home-based R&D to local market needs to a much more important role of creating new know-how, often related to the low-cost environments in which these R&D sites are created.

The 21st Century Artist

Globalization in the mid 19th Century provided both threats and opportunities for contemporary artists. While some artists tried to cling to established methods and behaviours, we have demonstrated how others adapted to the new world through adoption, integration and fusion. These global artists provide valuable lessons for today's managers, and becoming a truly global business leader will require a willingness to explore, to experiment and to be open to the fusion of new concepts and approaches. While the modern business leader might be armed with a laptop computer and Blackberry rather than a painting palette and easel, the opportunity to be part of the *avant-garde* of global management practice awaits. Are you ready to be the van Gogh, Gauguin, or Pablo Picasso of 21st Century business?

Additional Literature

Bakker, N. and Jansen, L. (2010) *The Real van Gogh: The Artist and His Letters*, London: Thames & Hudson.

Friedman, T. (2006) *The World is Flat: A brief history of the globalized world in the twenty-first century*, New York: Penguin Books Ltd.

Gauguin, P., Guerin, D. and Levieux, E. (1996) *Writings of a Savage PB: Paul Gauguin*, Da Capo Press.

Kupp, M. and Anderson, J. (2009) *Celtel Nigeria, ESMT Case Study: Case A and Case B*, ESMT-309-00(96/97)-1.

Kupp, M., Anderson, J. and Moaligou, R. (2009) Lessons from the Developing World, *The Wall Street Journal*, 17 August.

Reckhenrich, J., Anderson, J. and Kupp, M. (2009) Art Lessons for the Global Manager, *Business Strategy Review*, **20**(1): 50–57.

Richardson, J. (2007) *Life of Picasso Vols 1–3*, Knopf.

Stepan, P. (2006) *Picasso's Collection of African and Oceanic Art: Masters of Metamorphosis*, Munich: Prestel Verlag.

CHAPTER 6

Koons
Made in Heaven, Produced on Earth: Creative Leadership – The Art of Projection

I think one of the reasons why 'Rabbit' is an iconic work, is because it's so chameleon. This type of chameleon quality is what works need, because they have to continue to change and transform and meet the needs of the viewer

—Jeff Koons

Introduction

Leadership is of central importance in today's business world. After analysing, conceptualizing and evaluating, executives have to implement and get the company moving in the right direction. And here leadership comes into play. How can managers affect the thoughts, feelings and behaviours of a significant number of individuals in a way that strategies are flawlessly and passionately executed across an organization? Leadership also extends beyond the organization – it relates to how an individual manager can become recognized as a leader in their chosen *field* of business. Think of internationally recognized business leaders such as Anita Roddick, Richard Branson, Steve Jobs or Jack Welch. These leaders are not only acknowledged for what they have achieved through their respective careers at The Body Shop, Virgin Group, Apple and GE, but also for what they have come to represent as *embodiments* of certain business values. For a business leader to gain truly global credibility, not only must this embodiment be accepted *within* the organization, but the leader must also strive for recognition across a much *wider* sphere of influence. It is this more integrative approach of communication, behaviour and aspiration that can be termed "leadership *projection*".

There are an innumerable number of books and articles on the characteristics of business leaders that contribute to organizational success. Dimensions of leadership effectiveness include personality traits, cognitive and emotional skills and capabilities, passion, integrity and persuasion skills. The last of these traits – persuasion – has drawn significant attention in recent leadership literature, and it is widely acknowledged that a successful leader should be good at persuading others to identify with and then passionately implement the organization's strategies.

Persuasion is built upon the ability of leaders to establish credibility, and then to communicate key messages that drive commitment. Story-telling is a critical part of communicating these key messages; not delivered through sterile presentations, but rather through compelling narratives that engage and excite an audience. But while telling a good story is essential it surely is not sufficient. To build credibility it is equally crucial that the leader should embody the stories he or she tells in his or her life; the story should be true to the teller. And for a business leader to gain truly global credibility, not only must this embodiment be accepted within the organization, but the leader must also strive for recognition across a much wider sphere of influence – leadership *projection*.

Leadership projection is well understood in the world of art. Picasso is the artist who most frequently comes to mind when we ask an audience the question: who was the most creative genius of visual art in the 20th Century? If we ask who best represents the Pop Art movement, Andy Warhol is invariably cited as the true founder of that art approach in the 1970s. Warhol himself understood clearly the concept of leadership projection in an emerging artistic genre, and unashamedly projected himself as the leader of Pop Art. In this chapter we will take a close look at Jeff Koons, another successful and highly controversial contemporary artist. We explore the way in which story-telling linked to his artwork has been the key element of the way he has *projected* himself as a credible leader in the world of contemporary art. Koons' work receives worldwide recognition and is shown in virtually every major museum of modern art. His works have sold for astronomical prices at auctions and through private dealers. In 2001, one of his three *Michael Jackson and Bubbles* porcelain sculptures sold for $5.6 million. On 14 November 2007, a magenta *Hanging Heart*, one of five produced by Koons in different colours, sold at Sotheby's New York for $23.6 million becoming, at the time, the most expensive artwork by a living artist ever auctioned.

We suggest that Koons' use of story-telling, and the manner in which he has come to embody the themes and concepts that he seeks to communicate through his artworks, present powerful lessons for managers as to how they can manage their own leadership projection. By looking at Koons, managers can better understand not only how to establish credibility and drive buy-in, but also how to project themselves as leaders in their respective fields of business endeavour.

The Beginning

Jeff Koons narrates his story as an artist by beginning in his childhood in the 1960s. Koons once said that from a very early age the only thing he was really prepared for was being an artist.

> *I am really fortunate when I got to art school that I ended up in that profession, which really can be the hub to all the disciplines in the world. I found art as vehicle, which connects philosophy, sociology, with physics and aesthetics. It is wonderful to participate in this dialogue every day.*

Born in York, Pennsylvania in 1955, Koons started to take art lessons at the age of seven. Koons' father was an owner of a furniture shop, and showed the work of the young Koons in his store. The paintings were copies of old masters and the young child sold his first painting at the age of 11.

In 1972 Koons started to study at the Maryland Institute of Art in Baltimore and later at the School of the Art Institute in Chicago. In 1976 he graduated as Bachelor of Fine Arts and moved to New York. He started his first job to make a living at the Museum of Modern Art. "The Modern (MoMA) had such an impact on me, being able to study the collection every day, go through the galleries, come to the education department and seeing the films by Duchamp and Man Ray. My work is really based from the collection" (Jeff Koons, in Schneider, E. *et al.* (2009)).

Right from the beginning of his career Koons wanted to stay autonomous in order to realize his very own projects. Therefore, he worked as a Wall Street commodity broker, specializing in cotton, in order to finance his work, which was always costly to produce. While he typically downplayed this intermezzo, during this period he developed or deepened his understanding of the fundamental market mechanism, the way supply and demand set prices. Koons saw in that light the production of art, beside the creation of the idea, as a necessary investment in order to offer a high level of manufacturing quality of his work. This was to become a key success factor later in his work. He had worked together with appropriate technical specialists to realize his art projects, and the collaboration with craftspeople gave the naive appeal of many of his works the aura of professional manufacturing. This had been true from the renaissance era to modern art workshops like Andy Warhol's famous Pop Art "factory".

To appreciate the way in which Koons projected himself as a leader of contemporary art from the late 1970s, it is worthwhile considering each of his art series: "I tend to work very well by making groups of works and getting my narrative together, taking it as far as I can and then moving on". A deeper analysis of each of these series of artworks also demonstrates the manner in which Koons weaved an interlinked narrative across more than two decades of art production. This is close to what the sociologist Howard Gardner (1996) identifies as three universal story lines used by leaders to excite and gain buy-in from an audience:

1. Who am I – How life experience has shaped my individuality and character

2. Who are we – Demonstrate the values and behaviours of a group

3. Where are we going – Explains what is new, and creates a sense of excitement about direction.

A closer analysis of Koons' work reveals how he has leveraged each of these dimensions of effective story-telling as a broad narrative to link his various series together as a consistent whole.

Inflatables

Everything already exists in that world. I would go to a store and buy these inflatable flowers. I'd go to another store, a hardware store, and buy theses pre-cut glass mirrors, and I would display them. Or rather, these objects are just displaying themselves.

—Jeff Koons, in Schneider, E. *et al.* (2009)

When Koons moved to New York he gave up painting because he saw it as being too subjective. He developed a strong relation to Dada art from the 1920s and Surrealism. Koons wanted to connect to the everyday experience of his generation and to make work that connected and reflected the surrounding world, as he said, rather than focussing on his subjective, personal view. The earliest pieces were the *Inflatables* like the *Inflatable Bunny and Flower* from 1979. Koons said about these objects: "I've always liked Inflatables because they remind me of us. When breathing, we fill ourselves with air. This condition makes us vulnerable; it also keeps us in a state of constant change, inflating and deflating, taking in and putting out".

Koons bought these toys as brand new pieces from different shops and exhibited them with ready shaped mirrors he placed underneath the object and at the back. The artist produced these works at his tiny little apartment on East 4th Street. Visitors were challenged by a bombardment of "total" art, a disquieting yet at the same time jubilant floor to ceiling environment of aggressive commercial objects, an almost impenetrable density of plastic inflatables.

Important in his first series was the way he referred to art history. The *Inflatables* referred to Pop Art, but in a different way to Andy Warhol. While Warhol transferred popular items he saw or portraits he took as cheap, quick Polaroid images of famous people into graphic-abstract artworks, Koons referred to the Duchampian tradition of readymade art. Readymade artwork is an object which is instead of a painted or sculptured piece of art an already existing item often for everyday use. The artistic contribution is the change of context. Duchamp became well known for this concept and coined it when he presented his work

Fountain, a real urinal, at the commission of the Society of Independent Artists in New York in 1917. The commission rejected the object and Duchamp later became famous for his radical redefinition of art and art production afterwards.

The decision of Koons to work with buyable objects instead of producing original components, what he called subjective art, is how he developed his point of view in the complexity of art production in New York in the late 1970s. At that time, subjective art was established and accepted. While intuitively knowing that it was time for a new twist, Koons developed his story for an audience, galleries and art buyers that he felt were ready for a change. In this sense his approach was customized to a more sophisticated audience, but also backed by referring to a great tradition, taking the less sophisticated audience along.

The New

A lot of my work tends to have anthropomorphic qualities. When I was thinking about using vacuum cleaners, I thought that they're breathing machines. I always liked that quality of being like lungs. When you come into the world, the first thing you do is breathe to be able to live. I thought that for the individual to have integrity, the individual has to participate in life, and for the machine it is really the opposite. When they do function, they suck up dirt. The newness is gone. If one of these works were to be turned on, it would be destroyed

—Jeff Koons, in Schneider, E. *et al.* (2009)

During the early 1980s Koons continued with the concept of readymade when he started his series *The New*. All artworks were created around the term "new". Koons showed brand new vacuum cleaners and polishing machines displayed in plexiglass showcases and illuminated by neon light. Art critics interpreted theses pieces as monuments for the sterility of industrial production. Koons himself linked his series to art history. Regarding the piece *Hoover Celebrity III*, he explained that he simply wanted to arrange them like a picture of Piet Mondrian (1882–1944), a Dutch painter and icon during the Bauhaus area famous for his radical abstraction. But Koons thought after he made the first pieces that he was not contributing much to a Duchampian tradition and, therefore, decided to encase the vacuum cleaners as a reference to the way modern sculptures were often displayed. The objects were a distinctive selection. Koons was very aware of the history of the products and alluded with his choice to a famous American working myth: the Hoover man, the smallest business unit walking from door to door selling vacuum cleaners, way back in the 1950s.

While on the one hand Koons was clearly entering new territory with his *The New* series, he linked this series with his first *Inflatables* through several common themes. Both series stayed in the tradition of the readymade concept, which he constantly stressed in interviews. He was clearly shaping a consistent story and at the same time linking this story to his personal life as he openly discussed the things that influenced him like working at the New York Metropolitan Museum of Modern Art (MoMA).

This story was also powerful as in this still early phase of his career he was trying to connect to a rather sophisticated audience, the established art market players like galleries and museums. In that time Koons' work was not selling well and he started to work as a commodities trader on Wall Street, specializing in cotton, in order to stay independent and to finance his work. In 1979 Koons showed part of *The New* series at the window gallery at the New Museum of Contemporary Art, but had no follow-up exhibition.

Equilibrium

> *Equilibrium dealt with states of being that really don't exist, like a fish tank with a ball hovering in equilibrium, half in and half out of the water. This ultimate or desired state is not sustainable – eventually the ball will sink to the bottom of the tank. Then there were Nike posters, which acted as sirens that could take you under. I looked to the athletes in those posters as representing the artists of the moment, and the idea that we are using art for social mobility the way other ethnic groups have used sports. We were middle-class white kids using art to move up into another social class.*
>
> —Jeff Koons, in Schneider, E. *et al.* (2009)

In 1983 Koons started to create a body of work called *Equilibrium*. Koons wanted to show a more male aspect, as many people associated the vacuum cleaners with the feminine housewife of the 1950s. Through this work the artist displayed a kind of a darker side to the consumer world, more male oriented and more biological. Objects of the series were Nike posters of basketball stars, diving equipment cast in bronze and water tanks in which basketballs hovered in miraculous ways.

The whole series was following a strategy in which each piece played a particular part. The artwork *Dr. Dunkenstein*, a framed Nike poster for which Koons had asked the company's permission to use in the show, saw Koons as the star of the equilibrium show. The basketball star Darrell Griffith, whose nickname was "Dunkenstein", held a basketball divided exactly into two halves. This poster was a direct link to Koons' probably strongest artworks in the series, the 50/50 tanks. They were showcases filled half with water that contained basketballs. These pieces caused a sensation as the balls hovered exactly 50 percent over and 50 percent under the water, or in other completely filled tanks exactly in the middle. Koons received scientific support for this work from the Nobel prize winner Richard Feynman, who helped him with the complicated calculation of the composition of the water.

Koons created a story to tie the disparate artworks of the series together. He saw the *Dr. Dunkenstein* piece as a siren calling for equilibrium and the 50/50 tanks as objects for someone who desired a higher state of being. The diving equipment provided the tools to dive metaphorically into that specific state of mind.

Beyond the artistic approach there were several strategic elements to his story. First of all the story built on and yet expanded his previous narrative from *The New* series as it still related to readymade art and therefore helped the viewer (listener!) to accept the story as true to the teller (continuity, embodiment). At the same time Koons tapped into the scientific sphere by collaborating with Feynman, not just any scientist but a Nobel Prize winner. There was no doubt about the scientific authority of Feynman, which in turn supported the Koons story of authenticity.

Luxury Degradation

Luxury and Degradation gives a panoramic view of how the advertising industry targets an audience and how differently they'll use abstraction, depending on your income. They will feed you a certain level of abstraction; the more money comes into play, the more abstract. It is like they are using abstraction to debase you, because they always want to debase you. Like taking people into the ghetto and trying to sell them booze or making them show aggression.

—Jeff Koons, in Schneider, E. *et al.* (2009)

After the *Equilibrium* series Koons started to work on a new series called *Luxury Degradation* in 1986. This series was based upon alcohol advertisements and reflected the levelling out of society. When asked what inspired him to produce the series, Koons told the story of when he had walked down 5th Avenue and found a Jim Beam decanter train in a shop. That object attracted him because he saw it very much in the tradition of readymade art. He chose the train to become an artwork in the series but transformed it by using a different material. Koons decided to use stainless steel, a material pots and pans are made off and which had a more common and everyday life aspect compared to the classical material of sculptures bronze. He used that material for different objects around the topic of alcohol. Through the use of the material the items became objects of faked luxury. Other artworks of the series were big advertisement billboards, which he reprinted on the original pressure plates with special oil colour on canvas.

What attracted Koons was the way that emotion was key in the advertisement industry and that for different income levels this emotion was communicated differently, mainly through different levels of abstraction. By changing the context and putting degradation to the title of the series, Koons gave this story an ambiguous twist. Looking at the plain surface of the artworks, they looked perfect and slick. The term degradation and the way in which Koons displayed the artworks broke the clean surface.

Koons was criticized by artist colleagues and art critics that through the *Luxury Degradation* series he mainly targeted and served rich people. They were clearly missing a critical statement about society in his art production, which was very common in the 1980s. So, while the response to this series was quite controversial, it is noteworthy to look at the development of the Koons projection, at his story. There were a lot of elements which supported a certain sense of continuity, for example the way he continuously related his art to already existing concepts like the readymade art or the use of advertising posters, Nike posters in his *Equilibrium* series and now alcohol advertisements.

Being at that time already "validated" as an established artist, Koons had to extend his reputation and reach through a network of galleries, art dealers, art collectors and museums to cement his success. To build this network, this organization, he needed continuity as his story had to speak to a growing number of institutions and people. At the same time he needed to give his story a new twist. He did that by introducing new materials and also by the way he opened to ambiguity.

Statuary

Statuary presents an overall view of society: on one side there is Louis XIV and on the other side there is Bob Hope. If you put art in the hands of a monarch, it will reflect his ego and eventually becomes decorative. If you put it in the hands of the masses, it will reflect mass ego and eventually be-come decorative. If you put art in the hands of Jeff Koons, it will reflect my ego and eventually become decorative.

—Jeff Koons, in Schneider, E. et al. (2009)

Koons continued to work in stainless steel through the series *The Statuary* in 1986. The series was shown in the Sonnabend Gallery in New York as part of a group exhibition. Together with other artists, who all had a new approach to sculpture, sociologically-grounded abstraction and explorations of commodity culture in common, the show aimed to be the next new big thing, after the Neo-Expressionism way of painting. Koons was seen among these "hot" artists as the most interesting and accomplished one.

In producing the series Koons again used an overall principle to link the art pieces. He wanted to show the freedom modern artists had achieved, starting from around the period of the French Revolution when many artists broke free from the patronage of the church. The *Statuary* showed an enormous range of figures. All objects were rooted in kitsch aesthetic but had a clear social refer-ence. Koons showed a figure of the comedian Bob Hope, a very mass relate prole-tarian type, and also a bust of Louis XIV. *The Rabbit* was the most personal piece of *Statuary*. It was dedicated to Koons' erotic fantasies and he wanted to show his own relevance to the concept of readymade. *The Rabbit* became the most well known piece of the series.

In this series Koons shifted focus. While his *Equilibrium* series was still a more critical, outside view on society, he positioned *Statuary* as being part of mass culture, instead looking at it from outside. Koons pushed the acceptance of mass-market art and mass-taste as an inherent part of modern culture and the insight that people love – often in secret – the banal things of life as well as the so called objects of high culture that they were trained to accept as "important" to get closer to the taste and desire of his viewers. This was a move to strengthen the emotional side of his art.

Kiepenkerl

When I made the piece it was a total disaster. A foundry made it, and when they pulled the stainless steel out of the oven to knock the ceramic shell off, they banged it up against the wall while it was still molten. Every aspect of the piece was bent and deformed. Either I had to pull out of the exhibition or I had to give this piece radical plastic surgery. I decided on the radical surgery. We had a specialist brought in who was absolutely phenomenal with steel. He could do anything by rebending and reconverting the shapes to fit back together again. This work liberated me. I was free now to work with objects that did not preexist.

—Jeff Koons, in Schneider, E. et al. (2009)

In 1987 Koons was invited to the exhibition "Sculptural Projects – Münster" in Germany. For him, as a young artist starting to show his work internationally, this show was very important. Beside the five-year turn of the "Documenta" in Kassel, the exhibition in Münster was one of the most recommended art projects worldwide. All invited artists worked in close relation to specific architectural situations in Münster. This made the show unique. Koons went to Münster and saw the *Kiepenkerl* statue in the middle of an old town square. He got to know the community of Münster as being very dedicated to the story of the *Kiepenkerl* that represented the independence of the Münster middle class as an agrarian based community back in the 19th and early 20th Centuries.

Koons decided to take the bronze sculpture and to recast it into stainless steel as he thought it would meet people's economical understanding and independence in a different and more modern way. What the artist found attractive about the sculpture was obvious. Similar to the artworks from the *Statuary* series, the *Kiepenkerl* had a historical and sociological background. The figure was charged with meaning and emotions and spoke to the "simple man on the street". Koons' choice was intuitively right. There was much emotional discussion among the townspeople of Münster about whether it was right to turn a symbol of such proud and independent attitude into something so modern. The emotionalization of the historical background was the central point of the artwork.

Banality

These images are aspects from my own, but everybody's cultural history is perfect, it can't be anything other than what it is – it is absolute perfection. Banality was the embracement of that.

—Jeff Koons, in Schneider, E. et al. (2009)

In 1988 Koons decided to go to Europe in order to produce his next series *Banality*. With their long traditions of craftsmanship places like Italy and Germany were perfect locations, providing him with the opportunity to work with different materials. Koons decided to work with porcelain and wood, as he liked the "spiritual" quality of the materials.

Koons created different images of spirituality, like the sculpture of *St. John the Baptist*. Through this series he projected the idea that people need, from time to time, the confidence of a theological figure to let go of things, which in his words was "an act of banality". Banality was described by Koons as a concept of self-acceptance and the way that people deal with cultural guilt and shame. The Michael Jackson sculptures were at the core of the series. The nearly life sized porcelain figures, generously covered with gold, showed the famous singer holding his beloved chimpanzee Bubbles in his arms. Michael Jackson was perfect as a topic for *Banality*, because the pop-star figure embodied so many projections like popularity, innocence and animals. The figure represented, for Koons, a modern interpretation of the Renaissance type of Michelangelo's marble *Pieta* sculpture.

With the *Banality* series Koons also tried to connect to other artists to make them – through the concept of banality – embrace the power of open-minded communication. He stated that the traditional dialogue through art had become manipulative; projecting what is right or wrong. Koons tried to establish through his work a dialogue about the power and influence of art. He claimed artists should use all the creative tools like advertising, communication and manipulation, but had to be conscious of the kind of "moral" interactions with their communities. Koons himself didn't hesitate to walk the talk and produced a series of advertisements for the *Banality* exhibition showing himself in different provocative postures, all related to the idea of banality.

The audience was divided into fans and strict opponents, who claimed that Koons played with cheap emotions. Koons' story about banality had several important elements. He again clearly positioned his approach on a background of art history, in this case even on theological history heavily referring to Christian symbols. This clearly helped him to take his audience with him from one series to the next, giving them a sense of continuity. This was of course becoming more and more important as he was continuously building his reputation. This continuity also helped him build credibility, showing that he embodied his story, being true to his story and working on it in more detail. In this regard it was also important that he actively reached out to other artists, on the one hand communicating with them and on the other hand communicating to his audience that he clearly belonged to a set of established and known artists. At the same time Koons gave his story a new twist by working with porcelain and wood, materials he had not worked with before. In order to support this shift he moved to Europe and connected with the strong European craftsmanship tradition.

Made in Heaven

I'm dealing with the subjective and the objective. Modernism is subjective. I use modernism as a metaphor for sexuality without love as a kind of masturbation. And that's modernism.

—Jeff Koons, in Schneider, E. *et al.* (2009).

In 1989 Koons was approached by the Whitney museum to create an artwork as part of their upcoming exhibition "Image World", which should address the role of media in contemporary art. Koons decided to make a billboard designed like a film advertisement. He used an image of Ilona Staller "Cicciolina", an Italian porn-star actor who became famous for being part of the Italian parliament from 1987–1991, as the basis for his billboard. After seeing her in a men's magazine he immediately contacted her, met her in a discotheque and persuaded her to do a photo shoot in Rome. During the session he positioned himself next to Cicciolina in the exact same pose as he had seen her in the magazine. He called the piece *Made in Heaven* and it looked just like a billboard announcing a film starring the two actors Cicciolina and Jeff Koons. The artist fell in love with her and the two married. Koons said that he met his wife as a readymade and he produced a whole series around the love affair, using *Made in Heaven* as the headline, with artworks including sculptures of the couple making love and close-up photographic images of genitalia during intercourse.

This series reiterated the theme of "guilt and shame", this time referring to the way people experience their body, lust, sex and pornography. This topic was especially hot in the US from 1985 when Ronald Reagan established the Meese committee to investigate "cultural decline through the pornographic film industry". The debate had its peak in 1989 with the exhibition of Robert Mapplethorpe's erotic photography through the influential institution National Endowments of the arts. Koons was, with his *Made in Heaven* series, right in the centre of this conflict. But differently from other artists who created very critical work, like Andres Serrano's photo *Piss Christ*, in order to attack the establishment, Koons used a different approach. All things in *Made in Heaven*, the requisites, the clothing, the colours, were deeply rooted in middle class taste. However, instead of criticizing he chose a form of glorification to display his objects.

With the new series Koons found himself a new topic, which was widely debated at that time mainly in the US. But he anchored his story in several ways to his previous work. He repeated the overall theme of "guilt and shame", which he also exploited in the *Banality* series, and he explicitly drew reference to a wide range of artists and art themes like the Renaissance artist Masaccio and his work *Expulsion from Paradise*, the 18th Century sculptor Cannova and his famous artwork *Kiss*. He also connected his works to his own beginnings and the way he used readymade. This all strengthened his central story of "what you see is not what it is". The relationship with Cicciolina was not easy and the couple broke up after about a year.

Puppy

Inside, the Puppy is like a church. It is a shape like a bell tower, going up. Absolutely beautiful and pristine. I wanted the piece to deal with the human condition, and this condition in relation to God. I wanted to be a contemporary Sacred Heart of Jesus.

—Jeff Koons, in Schneider, E. *et al.* (2009)

Koons was not invited to the prestigious "Documenta" exhibition in Kassel Germany in 1992. The approach of the "Documenta" was to be radical and critical, but Koons was not acknowledged by the art-*avant-garde* due to his portrayal of the values and affections of middle class displayed through his *Banality* and *Made in Heaven* series. So it was a special triumph for him that his work *Puppy*, exhibited in a show close to Kassel, was the highlight of that "Documenta" summer.

Koons produced his *Puppy* sculpture, a shape of a Highland Terrier, for the garden sculpture show in Arolsen, Germany. Through this artwork the artist summarized what he had learned about Baroque and Rococo style in the *Banality* show. The size of the sculpture, 12 × 12× 6 metres, exceeded the dimensions of any of Koon's preceding artworks. The sculpture was made out of stainless steel, combined with a watering system for the flowers which were planted around the steel construction. Koons said that the artwork was very much about control, as there were 60,000 decisions to be made. "But control is not everything", he said, "What you have to do is to walk away, let go of human control and give it in the hands of nature and so the process of creation starts. Some of the plants will dominate others and in that way the sculpture displays the circle of life and death." In 1995, the sculpture was re-erected at the Museum of Contemporary

Art in Sydney, Australia. The piece was later purchased by the Solomon R. Guggenheim Foundation in Bilbao, where it was installed on the terrace outside the museum.

With *Puppy* Koons told a story again, and on a very emotional level. Everybody, according to Koons, had at least once in his or her life (probably as a child) a relationship with a small animal. Everything in the artwork, the choice of the shape of the puppy, the sheer incredible size and the beauty of the flowers, was chosen to please the viewer. To emotionalize an artwork, which was (only) close to the "Documenta", was a strategic decision. Koons knew that at the end of a show everything is measured by the hard fact of the number of visitors achieved. His goal was to hit the taste of the masses, and he succeeded in this objective.

Celebration

Celebration developed into a huge body of work that was going to be exhibited at the Guggenheim in New York. So the project demanded more work and time than a normal gallery exhibition. Then we ran into financial problems. It's not that I didn't do my work, or that I was being too obsessive about it. At the end of the day, the problem came down to increased costs for fabrication that were beyond our control. I believe in art morally. When I make an artwork, I try to use craft as a way, hopefully, to give the viewer a sense of trust. I never want anybody to look at a painting, or to look at a sculpture, and to lose trust in it somewhere.

—Jeff Koons, in Schneider, E. *et al.* (2009)

In 1994 Koons started to do a body of work called *Celebration*. The artist worked with a new readymade approach, modelling toy sculptures out of inflatable balloons. These popular toys became the prototype for new big steel sculptures like the *Balloon Dog*, *The Hanging Heart* and *Cracked Egg*. Some of the sculpture motives were transferred to oil paintings like *Tulips*, a 282 cm × 312 cm oil painting.

All of the artworks in this series appeared to be hyper-real and slick. Especially the oil paintings showed a super realistic aspect of transparency of the displayed material and the way in which the light reflexes were painted. Differently from other parts of Koons work, like *Equilibrium*, this series didn't have a conceptual framework. The objects displayed more of a panoramic overview of Koons iconography. Pretty much like classical church painting icons from the 16th Century like lilies, doves and crosses, which were "readable" for the masses, Koons created his own cosmos with eggs, flowers, diamond rings or abstract animal shapes.

The new steel sculptures opened a new market segment for Koons. Many communities in the US and Europe acquired them as decorative objects to upgrade town squares, garden architecture or fountains. The artist received varied reactions to his work. For instance the critic Amy Dempsey described the *Balloon Dog* as "an awesome presence . . . a massive durable monument". Jerry Saltz at artnet.com spoke enthusiastically of being "wowed by the technical virtuosity and eye-popping visual blast" of Koons' art. Others, such as the renowned art critic Robert Hughes, were much more critical, comparing the contemporary art scene with show business and stating that Koons represented "an extreme and self-satisfied manifestation of the sanctimony that attaches to big bucks . . . He has the slimy assurance, the gross patter about transcendence through art, of a blow-dried Baptist selling swamp acres in Florida. And the result is that you can't imagine America's singularly depraved culture without him". (*The Guardian* 30 June 2007).

The celebration series had an incredible impact on Koons' way of production. He was so much dedicated to perfection that he was not satisfied with many results. Koons claimed that he produced nearly 30 sculptures (which were scrapped) in the production line of the balloon flowers and *Balloon Dog* until he was satisfied. The oil paintings took up to three years to finish. The original planned exhibition at the Guggenheim for 1996 was postponed and finally cancelled. Koons ran into enormous financial problems in order to finish the work and to fund his workshop and assistants. Some gallery owners sold works from the series below the actual production cost, and Koons was forced to make financial arrangements with some collectors in order to pre-finance his ongoing work.

From a business point of view *Celebration* was a disaster. But Koons was following his vision of perfection, believing that the charm of his art and the emotional effect of perfectness, the "wow" moment of the visitor, could be destroyed if he could not deliver the artwork to the high standards he had achieved through the years.

Easyfun; Easyfun-Ethereal; Popeye, Hulk Elvis

My Easyfun-Ethereal paintings are very layered. My interest has always been to create art that can change with any culture or society viewing it. When I look at the paintings and realize all the historical references, it's as if, for a moment, all ego is lost to meaning.

—Jeff Koons, in Schneider, E. *et al.* (2009)

In 1999 Koons started, while still finishing the *Celebration* series, a new series of paintings titled *Easyfun* and later, for a show at the Guggenheim Berlin, *Easyfun Ethereal*. These series seemed to be an answer to the complicated production process of *Celebration*. While *Easyfun* was dedicated mostly to images of toys, the *Easyfun-Ethereal* series used parts of magazine advertisings. Koons created computerized collages which combined bikinis (with the bodies removed), parts of the human body, food and parts of landscapes. The original designs were transferred to large canvases and painted in a photorealistic way by his workshop. Koons put into these works many references to art history, with elements of Warhol, Dali and other renowned 19th and 20th Century artists. Critics described the paintings as irritating images where childish enjoyment and adult sexual desire were combined together in a weird way. The other series *Popeye* and *Hulk Elvis*, started in 2002, followed the same basic principles as *Easyfun-Ethereal*. The paintings and sculptures of these two series were playful and unbiased combinations of various objects. A lobster, an inflatable object cast in aluminium, could be combined with a chair, a paper basket, a log or a rubber swim ring. In the painting *Olive Oyl* the artist put Superman side by side with Popeye. Koons was back where he once had started. He followed his roots of readymade art, inflatables and icons of popular culture. "I find that the work for myself is more and more minimal. I've returned to the readymade. I've returned to really enjoying thinking about Duchamp. This whole world seems to have opened itself up again to me, the dialogue of art" (Jeff Koons, in Schneider, E. *et al.* (2009)).

All these series demonstrated how Koons created, after the challenges of the *Celebration* series, a straight line of production in his work. His main topic became the lightness of the arrangement of modular pieces in combination with perfect standard of production. The quality of the surface became so strong that visitors of his shows always wanted to touch the objects. It seemed to be as though Koons wanted to communicate that everything appears at the surface and that is what counts. Compared to other series like *Equilibrium* or *Made in Heaven* all of Koon's later series seemed to be more open and playful. The artist related these works to his surrealistic beginning, by combining non-coherent things to a surprising new artistic language of images: "I don't believe that you can create art. But I believe what will lead you to art is to trust in yourself, follow your interests. That will take you to a very metaphysical state". Sometimes it is hard to say whether Koons is the master or a medium of his art.

Managerial Implications

Leadership projection is an integrative approach of communication, behaviour and aspiration that not only drives buy-in and passionate followership of a leader's vision but also provides the leader with wider recognition across an industry or sphere of public life. It is widely acknowledged that a leader has to be a good story-teller and that it is equally crucial that the leader embodies that story in his or her life. A leader's stories have to wrestle with those that are already in the minds of the target group or audience. Therefore, it is important for leaders to know their stories, to get them straight, to communicate them effectively and to embody the stories that they tell. They should do so consistently and over a period of time represented by years rather than weeks or months.

According to Gardner, here are three universal story lines used by leaders to excite and gain buy-in from an audience: "Who am I?", "Who are we?" and "Where are we going?". Among the various elements of a good story it seems critical that it is true to the teller, that it balances the "I" and the "we" and that it not only provides background but also frames the future. Great story-telling builds on stories that are already known and allows the audience to synthesize them in new ways.

Throughout his career Koons has referred to his personal roots and his passion for art that stemmed from his early childhood. His story of "Who am I?" weaves a narrative from his childhood experiences of selling his artworks door-to-door and the sale of his first painting at the age of 11, to his early work experience at the Metropolitan Museum of Art and the hardships and tribulations of establishing his Soho studio. He has also provided striking and sometimes controversial insights into his own personal values. In exhibiting the *Banality* series Koons said: "In the Banality work, I started to be really specific about what my interests were. Everything here is a metaphor for the viewer's cultural guilt and shame." Commenting on his *Made in Heaven* series Koons provided even deeper insights into his personal views on guilt and shame: "Sex with love is a higher state. It's an objective state, in which one lives and enters the eternal, and I believe that's what I showed people. There was love there. That's why it wasn't pornographic."

Koons has positioned his narrative of "Who are we?" for the key consumers of contemporary art – consumers (viewers), collectors and galleries of modern art. In each and every one of his series he has referred to art history, claiming that this provides a strong connection between his work and humanity. He has quoted Piet Mondrian, and set himself in the readymade tradition of Marcel

Duchamp. He has referred to Renaissance artists like Masaccio and his work *Expulsion from Paradise* and to the 18th Century sculptor Cannova and his famous artwork *Kiss* in his *Made in Heaven* series. The *Lips* painting in his *Easyfun-Ethereal* series was in some parts very close to Salvador Dali's portrait of Mae West. Other parts of the painting were nearly art quotations, like "The eye in the middle", a link to Man Ray's famous artwork *The Eye of the Beholder* showing a metronome with a glued eye on the metronome pendulum. Even his porcelain Michael Jackson sculpture that was part of the *Banality* series represented, for Koons, the "Renaissance type of the Pieta transferred to modernity." Koons said, "I wanted to have spiritual authoritarian figures there, in the Garden of Eden so that people wouldn't be afraid to just give into the banality. The little animated bird on his shoulder is like the Holy Spirit, and there's a miniature pony instead of a donkey, but this is like Christ." His reference to art history has been a consistent and very important element in his story, part of his leadership projection to place himself alongside historically significant art figures from the Renaissance onwards.

Koons has also helped his audience to understand how contemporary art is evolving, and has explained the manner in which he has shaped 20th and 21st Century art trends – the "where are we going?" dimension of leadership projection. In his narratives about his different series Koons has identified how his works link to art history, but also how his approach represents something creative – something new. His *Inflatables* series referred to Pop Art and clearly built upon the traditions of Andy Warhol. But while Warhol transferred popular items he saw into graphic-abstract artworks, Koons merged Pop Art and Duchampian readymade art. Speaking about the historical roots, but also the innovation of his approach, Koons has said, "To me the major artistic dialogue of the 20th century was between subjective and objective art. Subjective art is about the self and personal experience, when you're working physically with your own hands. Objective art is like the art of Duchamp or Warhol that's more about communal experience. To actually physically work on something, you can get lost in yourself. It ends up being just about what you dreamt the night before." In this quote Koons positions his own personal subjective approach, linked to but distinctive from what has come before. He clearly positions himself as an equal to Duchamp and Warhol, and an artist who deems himself worthy of recognition by future art historians.

Persuasion is built upon the ability of leaders to establish credibility and then to communicate key messages that drive commitment, and Jeff Koons has succeeded in persuading a wide international audience that he is a "leader" in the sphere of contemporary art. While art critics are divided on the merits of his approach, his artworks are now exhibited in many of the world's most respected public galleries of modern art and individual pieces can sell for tens of millions of dollars – demonstrating the degree of buy-in and commitment from key constituencies. Koons has built credibility through a remarkably consistent embodiment of the stories he has told, linked to the series of works he has produced. He has projected himself as an artist of the highest merit and has unashamedly linked his own career to those of some of the most widely recognized artists of all time. According to art critic Robert Hughes, "Koons really does think he's Michelangelo and is not shy to say so. The significant thing is that there are collectors, especially in America, who believe it."

While Jeff Koons' two-decade long narrative is far from being perfect, and certainly has its flaws, we believe that aspiring executives can draw insights from his story. As Koons' success demonstrates, in an increasingly crowded and competitive environment for talent the concept of "projection" is at the heart of creative leadership for the 21st Century.

Additional Literature

Barling, J., Weber, T. and Kelloway, E.K. (1996) Effects of transformational leadership training on attitudinal and financial outcomes: A field experiment, *Journal of Applied Psychology*, **81**: 827–832.

Barnes, E. (2003) What's your story? *Harvard Management Communication Letter*, 3–5 July.

Bass, B.M., Avolio, B.J. and Goodheim, L. (1987) Biography and the Assessment of Transformational Leadership at the World-Class Level, *Journal of Management*, **13**: 7–19.

Conger, J.A. (1998) The Necessary Art of Persuasion, *Harvard Business Review*, May–June: 85–95.

Eagly, A.H. (2003) The rise of female leaders, *Zeitschrift für Sozialpsychologie*, **34**: 123–132.

Fuller, J.B., Patterson, C.E.P., Hester, K. and Stringer, S.Y. (1996) A quantitative review of research on charismatic leadership, *Psychological Reports*, **78**: 271–287.

Gardner, H. (1995) *Leading Minds: An Anatomy of Leadership*, New York: Basic Books.

Guber, P. (2007) The Four Truths of the Storyteller, *Harvard Business Review*, December: 53–59.

House, R.J., Spangler, W.D. and Woycke, J. (1991) Personality and Charisma in the United-States Presidency—A Psychological Theory of Leader Effectiveness, *Administrative Science Quarterly*, **36**: 364–396.

Hughes, R. (2004) That's show business, *The Guardian*, 30 June 2004.

Schneider, E., Sischy, I., Siegel, K. and Werner Holzwarth, H. (2009) *Jeff Koons*, Köln: Taschen Verlag.

CHAPTER 7

Paik
Global Groove –
Innovation through
Juxtaposition

Our life is half natural and half technological. Half-and-half is good.

—Nam June Paik

Introduction

In 1974, the artist, Nam June Paik (Paik) created one of the most famous video art-works the *Television Buddha*, which is still referred to as "an icon of the genre". Just prior to the inauguration of his fourth show in Gallery Bonino, New York, Paik was still missing a piece. He had an idea to create a short video clip of an antique Buddha statue. Juggling with the idea of incorporating video material in his show, which in those times was a new and developing art form, Paik came up with the idea of producing a closed circuit installation, placing the bronze Buddha in front of a television, where he could see himself. By choosing a closed circuit installation, Paik was not only able to bridge photography and video (although it was a video nothing moved and the work thereby played on the term "moving pictures") but also to bridge East and West, philosophy and technology, past and present. Through the *Television Buddha*, Paik added a cornerstone to a whole new art form called "video art". The *Television Buddha* became the object no artist after him could ignore and the piece became a label for Paik and his art. Later he showcased the *Television Buddha* in many different variations.

During the late 1960s and 1970s, video art was just beginning to take off. Video technology then was in its infancy, not really developed on a consumer level and just too expensive. It was Paik who sensed that video technology would become more accessible, and would enable innovative artworks and new creative possibilities – just as the invention of film technology by the brothers Lumiere had done after 1895. Pushing video art was by all means risky in 1974, as the new technology was far from being accepted as a mainstream art form. But at the same time Paik clearly sensed the unique opportunity every new technology provides first movers, so neglecting it was not an option for him.

It is not only artists, but also business people who face such dilemmas. Life seems to be an endless stream of trade-offs, either–ors, decisions for cost or differentiation, lefts or rights. Although there is truth in this, one would wish there was a third option – the winning combination – which would enable us to opt for the best of both worlds, meaning the synthesis of two opposing options. For example, in the case of Paik it is not photography or video art, still or moving, Eastern philosophy or Western technology, but a new approach to exploiting new possibilities built upon what has come before.

Today's business environment continuously forces us to explore this kind of juggling with potentially opposing ideas and conflicts – the process of juxtaposition. Born in Korea, educated as a musician in Asia and Europe, possessing US citizenship, producing artwork, Paik incorporates the idea of innovation through juxtaposition. Looking at Paik, managers can understand the potential of juxtaposition, of holding opposable positions in mind in order to envision and to create new solutions. It is the core of creativity. In approaching Juxtaposition, managers need to acknowledge three critical dimensions: they have to face complexity as resource for unknown ideas; they have to orchestrate the creative potential within the organization; and they have to find a way to emotionalize the ideas and solutions which emerge in order to get their message across. Juxtaposition, with its three dimensions, is a skill which becomes important in turbulent times, as more linear approaches to innovation simply do not deliver the desired results.

A Passenger from East to West

Paik's career as an artist can be seen as a truly global journey; and his influence upon the development of video art and television has been profound. In order to understand the specific and distinctive character of Paik's art, it is necessary to look deeper into his mercurial movements, beginning in Asia, going to Europe and then to the US. His shifting cultural interests, holding in mind various cultural concepts, led Paik to the kind of creative tension he needed to melt such influences into something new, something more than a simple combination.

From the point of view of the artistic material that Paik worked with, his complex career can be seen as a process, which started with his early interests in composition and performance. This impact strongly shaped his ideas for media oriented art at a time when the electronic moving image and media technologies were gaining a stronger impact in daily life. His remarkable career evoked a redefinition of broadcast television and transformed video into an artist's medium.

Paik's life as an artist was grounded in the politics and anti-art movement of the 1950s–1970s. This time was known for huge societal and cultural changes. Paik was able to follow a determined quest to combine the direct, expressive and conceptual power of performance art with the new technological possibilities developed from the growing television Industry. Hailing from the East, Paik was able to create a fresh view on European art and history, an early form of cultural crossover technique, and left a sustainable impact upon media in the late 20th Century.

The Beginning

Nam June Paik was born in 1932 in Seoul, Korea. He was the fifth son of a textile manufacturer. In 1950, his family had to leave Korea due to the war. They first moved to Hong Kong and later to Japan. Paik concluded his studies in Art History and History of Music with a thesis on Arnold Schönberg (1874–1951) in 1956 at the University of Tokyo. Soon after, he moved to Germany with the desire to understand the way of classical European composition and its modern tradition. From 1956–1958 he studied History of Music at Munich University. It was in Munich that he met the composer Karlheinz Stockhausen (1928–2007).

The year 1958 marked a very important point in Paik's life when he met John Cage (1912–1992). During that time, Cage was known to be the most influential experimental musician. Cage created works like the famous composition *4,33*, a piece of music where the player entered the stage, had to sit in front of the score and concentrate for 4.33 minutes without playing one single note. With Cage's strong interest in Buddhism (where all creation emerges out of silence), Paik met a familiar mind, who renewed modern music through his interest in Eastern culture. Cage's work was very profound for Paik's development. The complex mindset of Cage's thinking resonated with Paik's ongoing search and his longing to find a new approach that would eventually create new kinds of art experience.

In his early career, Paik developed "action" oriented pieces of music like the *Stockhausen's Originale*. He learned through Schönberg, Stockhausen and others the limits of serial composition and strictness. Paik went for a radical break from these modern techniques, and was influenced by various anti-art movements which circulated through Europe during those times. Artists like Joseph Beuys, Yves Klein, Claes Oldenburg, Christo and others questioned the idea of the "pure" art object and its lonely genius creator. Each day these artists explored many new artistic scenarios and experienced their impact. As a result, Paik found a place to continue and renew his self-definition as an artist.

The Fluxus Time

"I am tired of renewing the form of music . . . I must renew the ontological form of music in 'Moving Theatre' in the street, the sounds move in the street, the audience meets or encounters them 'unexpectedly'. The

beauty of moving theatre lies in this 'surprise a priori', because most of the audience is uninvited, not knowing what it is, why it is, who is the composer, the player, organizer"

—Nam June Paik (1963) The worlds of Nam June Paik, p. 17

The name Fluxus was taken from the Latin word which means "to flow". Fluxus as art movement consisted of an international network of artists, composers and designers and was the first real artist network after World War II. This group became famous for its blend of different media and disciplines. The unlimited positioning of artistic material aimed for a breakthrough of all kinds of unexpected and new art. Soon after founding the Fluxus movement in New York in 1962, through the artist George Maciunas, it was established in Germany, in the town Wiesbaden, by the "Internationale Festspiele Neuster Musik".

Fluxus aimed to integrate art into daily life experiences and social processes. "It is all about life and its influencing processes and not about the separation of art from life" (*medienkunstnetz*). The famous poet Emmett Williams once said: "Life is an artwork and the artwork is life". In the 1950s artists experimented with a broad approach and blurred the boundaries of art and society. Art was taking over a more active role by commenting on current social developments like the new economic development in Germany, called *Wirtschaftswunder*. Fluxus as an art movement aimed for a new definition of society, questioning the political and social environment after World War II with its tendency to neglect what had happened and the aim to return to normal. Fluxus drew a line to the revolutionary Dada movement of the early 20th Century that claimed in a famous statement that, "If middle class rationality was responsible for the horrific World War I, we declare unreasonableness to the real state of mind." Like Dada, Fluxus integrated all kinds of artistic materials in order to create real life experiences. Artists like Joseph Beuys used the Fluxus movement (he founded the "Fluxus Area West") in order to elaborate the radical different understanding and redefinition of art and developed the concept of the *Erweiterter Kunstbegriff* (enhanced term of art).

The Fluxus artists preferred to work with materials which were often easy to get hold of. It was not common to outsource parts of the creative process to commercial fabricators (very different from the modern "production lines" of Jeff Koons or Damien Hirst). The art movement preferred a "do-it-yourself" aesthetic and valued simplicity of style and production quality over complexity and perfection. Fluxus included a strong anti-commercialism sentiment. It favoured clearly the artist-centred creative practice and proclaimed that art could emerge in every life situation.

When Fluxus moved to Cologne from New York in the early 1960s, it was absorbed by a specific artistic and cultural atmosphere. Cologne became the most prominent art centre in Germany. The intention of "Fluxus Concerts" was to create a lively and holistic picture of society. The Fluxus artists aimed at reflecting society without compromising and tried to broaden the expectations and perspectives of the audience. The provoking aspects and attacks on the traditional values of the *Wirtschsftswunder* polarized the audience. Fluxus always wanted to influence the sociological and psychological level of society and be an element of communication. The complexity of the Fluxus concerts and the co-operation of different artists created new artistic interpretation. For instance, in one performance Paik was sitting very close to and in front of the cello player Charlotte Moorman, holding a string on his back, imitating the corpus of the cello, while Moorman, holding a cello stick, played literally on Paik as a musical instrument.

Music/Performance

Paik's ongoing experimental attitude and drive to constantly create crossover pieces of art was visible in most of his artworks: this led him to join the Fluxus movement. In the piece *Homage à John Cage*, first performed in 1959 at the Wilhelm's Gallery 22 in Düsseldorf, Paik used readymade audiotapes and perform elements. Paik produced audiotape recordings of himself, arranging on the tapes a mixture of piano playing and screaming, parts of classical music and additional sound effects. Paik was not satisfied with the tape sound and decided to integrate performance elements. In a related piece *Memories of the 20th Century: Marilyn Monroe* (1962), Paik used a phonograph cabinet and filled it with popular records, magazines and newspapers which announced the actress' death. In that way, Paik explored Monroe's mystique and death by examining the reflection through the popular media. The performance had its high moments when Paik played and smashed the records throughout the theatre, extending with his treatment of the record medium the idea of "playing" music.

In his *avant-garde* extravaganza, Paik performed *Zen for Head* and other works which engaged the artist in strong physical actions. In *Zen for Head*, Paik kneeled on the floor and dipped his tie into a big pot filled with black ink and then tried to draw a line on a long piece of paper. Paik's reference to the Zen practise where the student tries to break-through his or her mental corset of rationality seems a bit like an ironic comment to the Western world that was trying to understand this spiritual concept of the East. Paik's way of artistic self-discovery reached another level with his contribution to the concert "Originale" of Stockhausen, a multi-artist, multi-textual music theatre event. Stockhausen who was a crucial figure in the development of Paik described the artist's presence on the stage in the following way:

> Paik came onto the stage in silence and shocked most audience by his actions which were as quick as lightning. For example, he threw beans against the ceiling, which was above the audience and onto the audience. He then hid his face behind a roll of paper, which he unrolled infinitely slowly in breathless silence. Then, sobbing softly, he pressed the paper every now and then against his eyes and the paper became wet with tears. He screamed as he suddenly threw the paper into the audience and at the same moment he switched on two tape recorders with what was a sound montage typically of him, consisting of women's screams, radio news, children's noise, fragments of classical music and electronic sounds. At times he switched on an old gramophone with a record of Hayden's string quartet version of the 'Deutschlandlied'. Immediately after that at the back stage ramp he emptied a tube of shaving cream into his hair and smeared its content over his face, over his dark suit and down to his feet. He then slowly shook a bag of rice flour over his head. Finally, he jumped into a bathtub filled with water and dived completely underwater, jumped soaking wet to the piano and began a sentimental salon piece. He then fell forward and hit the piano keyboard several times with his head.
>
> —Karl Heinz Stockhausen, Essays 1952–1962, p. 29

Artist/Audience

As a typical feature of the Fluxus movement, Paik's performances aimed to cross the border between the artist and the audience. Therefore, play and coincidence became an important artistic feature. A piece of art was not understood as a finished piece, but only came alive through the performance and the interaction with the audience. In his first solo exhibition in 1963, "Exposition of Music–Electronic Television" at the gallery Parnass in Wuppertal, visitors played a crucial role in the piece – *Symphony for 20 Rooms*. The audience was directed to shape the artwork by playing audio tape machines, kicking objects in the room or listening to audio materials that Paik had combined from various sources. The artist mixed the installation of objects with the performance approach and tried to achieve the visualization of music much more than recording or playing music. This included semi prepared pianos. In the piece called *Klavier Integral* (*Piano*

Integral) a piano was decorated with barbed wire, dolls, photos, toys, a bra, smashed eggs and various other bizarre things which Paik added into the perform-ance and interaction with the piano. He scratched, splashed paint over the piano, covered it with different materials and so altered the shape of the instrument and its interiors. A dramatic extension of Paik's performances occurred when his artist colleague Joseph Beuys visited the exhibition. Beuys destroyed one of the pianos with an axe. The violation of the performance process and the transformation and destruction of a classical musical instrument altered in a radical way the protocols of performance art and the reception and understanding of an artwork.

Through these improvized actions, artists explored the boundaries of the medium and their audience. Paik's multifaceted scenarios displayed the fragility of permanence and the upheaval of his exile from Korea. The artist tried to develop his very own cultural identity by using various influences as well as observing the kind of unknown identity which emerged out of this clash. Paik drew this in a drawing called *Fluxus Island* in 1963. In *Fluxus Island*, surrounded by artist friends, he created his own separate world with which he always identi-fied himself and to which he always could return mentally. Through that world, he shaped his self-related and personal performance strategy. Paik was able to act fearlessly and be self-exposed on stage, expressing the freedom he had found in the Fluxus community. The artist acknowledged these friendships, developed from the early 1960s in various art projects. Paik hoped to place his thinking in a larger social and political context in order to better communicate his beliefs.

Music/Television

When Paik moved to New York his cross-cultural/cross-media thinking reso-nated with the multiple cultural influences there.

In 1986, Paik remarked:

> *In March 1963, while I was devoting myself to research on video, I lost my interest in action in music to a certain extent. After twelve performances of Karlheinz Stockhausen's "Originale", I started a new life from November 1961. By starting a new life, I mean that I stocked my whole library except those on Television technique into storage and locked it up I read and practised only electronics. In other words, I went back to the Spartan life of pre-college days . . . only physics and electronics*
>
> —Nam June Paik (1963) The worlds of Nam June Paik, p. 34

Paik's work with television began with an installation that was displayed in the Wuppertal exhibition "Exposition of Music–Electronic Television". The artist installed thirteen television monitors that lay on their backs and on their sides, and through this installation he altered the reception. With a technical trick he broke the standardized engineered television image. In *Zen for Television* he reduced the television picture to a horizontal line. Paik turned the monitor to the side and through this got a vertical line. Other television monitors were laid with their screens to the floor. In a piece called *Rembrandt Automatic* (1963) the television was turned on and projected a flickering light (an analogy to the flickering use of colours by Rembrandt) onto the floor. In that way, Paik disabled the normal function of the television and raised the object to a more abstract level. This redefinition and break from the normal use of a television set altered the viewer's attitude in a radical way, so that he or she had to look at the television as an object of its own, rather than a container for films. Another piece called *Point of Light* (1963) was an interactive installation. A radio pulse generator was placed on the television set. The visitor could turn the volume up and down and so the point of light in the centre became larger or smaller. In the prototype of *Participation Television* (1963) a microphone that could be switched on was connected to the television. When a visitor turned on the microphone and started to speak, the voice was translated into an explosive pattern of dots on the screen (technical games like that are produced nowadays as applications for the iPhone). Paik anticipated through this very playful approach the idea of active participation of the viewer (something that was not developed in television history until the late 1980s). He literally saw the television tube as a compositional device, a surface which by distortions and broadcast images could be altered. Paik aimed at using the television tube as an instrument to create images.

Humans/Machines

In 1964, when Paik moved to New York, he progressed to the next step of transition, from performance to media. The artist created his very first remote controlled robot called *Robot K-456* which was featured in his *Robot Opera* at the second Annual New York *avant-garde* Festival. The object was a mixture of all the technology Paik had used before. It was put together from various electronic components, wood, wire and foam rubber. The robot was able to move by radio control and had a humanoid shape with 2 legs, two arms, a rough form of a head and was 185 cm tall. The artwork had a kind of an improvized appearance, a style towards which Paik worked a lot and it later became his distinctive artistic mark.

Through *Robot K-456* Paik developed the prototype for the many human–robot sculptures he created later, all the way to his famous work-group *Family of Robot* in 1986. The prototype itself was an ambitious crossover of Paik's research of new technical possibilities and his experience with performance art. *Robot K-456* had an integrated audiotape machine that played speeches of John F. Kennedy and threw beans around when it rumbled around the exhibition space. In many ways this very first robot showed the tendency of Paik to juxtapose different options and thereby find new forms of art. The audiotapes with Kennedy's voice could be seen as his dedication to the new world and the new culture he had arrived in. The shape of the robot itself appeared a most playful way to present technology.

Paik wanted to humanize and foster the understanding of technology and the instruments of culture. Although Paik had used technology before (he always had and often spearheaded the exploration of options behind regular use), *Robot K-456* looked like a rough and funny collage or an assemblage, a kind of artwork which was created by the German artist Kurt Schwitters (1887–1948) who was very important for Paik's development. *Robot K-456* was a mixture of new Western technology (video, audio device, remote control technique), references to art history (assemblage technique of Schwitters and the playfulness of Dada art in the 1920s) and a blend of Paik's cultural Buddhist background and his experience of the Western way of living. His connection to Buddhism, which claims detachment as one of the highest mental states in spiritual development, opened for Paik the path to work with various artistic materials less seriously and more playfully. This quality helped Paik throughout his life to deal with the opponent artist colleagues he worked with to continuously create new forms of artwork.

Paik developed an approach which was based on juxtaposing seemingly opposing ideas or frameworks like technology and culture, humans and machines, and through these creating new ideas about technology. His curiosity and playful mind was constantly exploring new technical options and challenging them in order to create new ways for his art. He also played with his various cultural roots and cultural experiences. Above all, he was able to hold all these things in his mind at the same time, not judging which part has more meaning than another. During his career these various parts of his personality enabled him to create new artworks. Paik's different cultural backgrounds, his playful, unattached and inspired mind, his openness to technique and questions of culture made him one of the first modern "global players" in the newly invented and international art scene after World War II.

Technology/Sexuality

The real issue implied in 'Art and Technology' is not to make another scientific toy, but how to humanize the technology and electronic medium, which is progressing rapidly . . . Television Brassiere for Living Sculpture (Charlotte Moorman) is also one sharp example to humanize electronics . . . and technology. By using Television as bra . . . the most intimate belonging of a human being, we will demonstrate the human use of technology, and also stimulate viewers NOT for something mean but stimulate their fantasy to look for the new, imaginative and humanistic ways of using our technology

—Nam June Paik (1969) The worlds of Nam June Paik, p. 62

Paik's aim to question and display a humanized approach to technology led him to an experimental way to mix object making, performance actions, audiotape compositions, research of technology and the transformation and manipulation of television sets. It was through such an experimental attitude that Paik developed a broad artistic repertoire, from the early days of his career. He always explored different options rather than dedicate himself to one specific area. This attitude placed him in a very unique position giving him the freedom to develop radical artistic steps in order to fulfil his artistic mission.

One scope of Paik's performance and research was the role of the human body and his desire to integrate sexuality into music and performance. He used the performance to expose and explore, often through the use of subversive humour, the role of the erotic within the act of performance and their reception. He acknowledged female sexuality and the shape of the female body as a way to convey unconscious eroticism to the performance act on stage. These kinds of performance pieces tested the boundaries of the audience.

Paik explored the erotic humanized approach in his collaboration with Moorman, which began in 1963 when Moorman organized the first New York *Avant-Garde* Festival. Paik developed exclusively for her a set of extraordinary and elaborate pieces. Moorman was Paik's most important collaborator, who inspired, sustained and was actively engaged in the artist's milestone work in video and dramatic performance. It was a hit when Moorman performed Paik's *Opera Sextronique* (1967), a striptease while playing the cello at the Filmmakers Cinematheque in New York. This performance led to the arrest of Paik and Moorman and a scandal in the public media. Since then Moorman was called the "Topless Cello Player". Ironically, Paik himself had announced the performance in a programme note: "Why is sex a predominant theme in art and literature, prohibited ONLY in music?" Moorman was a tireless performer and absolutely dedicated to the art that she performed around the world. Paik created a remarkable set of video artworks for her and their collaboration drastically transformed the concepts of performance art and its interpretation.

In the piece *Television Bra for Living* (1969), which had its premier at the exhibition "Television as Creative Medium" at the Howard Wise Gallery, Moorman wore two television tubes inside plexiglass cases that were taped to her breasts during the performance. Paik created another piece for Moorman called *Television Cello* (1971), that was actually a form of a cello built out of three television sets (a big one at the top and the bottom and a small one in the middle). The musician played on a string that was assembled on the televisions in the same way as it is on a cello. It was the most radical work of their collaboration. The duo performed their interpretation of John Cage's composition *26'1.1499*, a conceptual piece of music (in such pieces Cage had given more instructions to the player on what to do than concrete lines of notes). Paik kneeling in front of Moorman, laid his head to her throat and held on his backside a single cello string. Moorman held Paik pretty much as the corpus of a cello and played with her cello bow on Paik's back.

Moorman stated that *Television Cello* was "the first advance in cello since 1600". In all these pieces, the television monitors showed videotapes or closed-circuit television footage, or were linked to strings of the cello to create an interaction between the images and the electronic sound. The strength of all these pieces came through Moorman's strong and charismatic presence. She had the ability to present the curious combinations of Paik's objects and video images with wit and straight-faced humour in the performances. As a result, she was able to contribute one of the particular features of Paik's video sculptures. Paik had the ability to humanize the medium and make it accessible as a tool for individual understanding and creative use. Through that approach the artist questioned television in its role as a mass entertainment instrument very early on. By turning television into an everyday personal and performance object, he pushed the technology to a human scale and form of expression. Paik's fascination with the female body, his longing to eroticize the music, his desire to manipulate the body of the performer, including his own, and his desire to run the performance act on a metaphorical level as a sexual act could only be realized by collaborating with Moorman.

Paik's work was built on hand fabrication of things that could break down into minute pieces and required repair. This became a strong feature in the performances with Moorman and underlined the idea of an ongoing process, because at every performance the object combination was different. The handcrafted objects had their own poetic expression with their wires, video decks and monitors. They conveyed Paik's quality of art production as the pure technique was used to create extraordinary stage settings in which Moorman performed. His collaboration with the musician met Paik's deep understanding of performance, the body as instrument and object of desire and video as a deformable medium that became an art form.

Electronics/Culture

The Television Synthesiser will enable us to shape the Television screen canvas

as precisely	*as Leonardo as freely as Picasso*
as colourfully	*as Renoir*
as profoundly	*as Mondrian*
as violently	*as Pollock*
as lyrically	*as Jasper Jones*

—Paik, 1969

The television objects Paik developed for the performance with Moorman later became single objects or installations like *Television Cross* (1968), the famous *Television Buddha* or the big video installation *Television Garden* (1977). To understand the complexity of these works, it becomes necessary to explore Paik's understanding of television technology as an art instrument. The artist tried to make television strange and unfamiliar and wanted to link the medium to the surprise and shock in his performances. Too often, in the opinion of Paik, television was taken for granted by consumers and was too familiar. Therefore, he dislodged the comfortable and uncritical view of television. After moving to the US, Paik began to develop his ideas about the transformation of television and its technology.

Paik opposed the idea of television as a defined and limited medium. He saw television more as something that must be explored as a process and tested as an object in the performances. Paik was able to question the power of conformity he experienced with television as a mass instrument. Paik believed in the idea of pure (or *avant-garde*) art that is conceived by the artist, is visible to those who are engaged with it and which ignores the onrushing and consuming forces of the art market place and consumer culture.

In the 1960s, artists nourished the idea of *avant-garde* as being a cultural elite and claimed that viewers had to develop an appropriate understanding. Paik, with his love for conceptual thinking and his playful attitude, once said: "I am a poor man from a poor country, so I have to be entertaining all the time". This was an ironic statement with a double meaning. On one hand he commented on the tendencies of consumption he observed in mass media and television as its instrument, on the other hand he pointed to the over intellectual tendencies of his artist colleagues.

Since 1961, Paik had dreamt about an affordable video device. In 1965, Sony launched a portable half-inch videotape recorder. This piece of technology enabled Paik to move his creative approach in multiple directions. For the first time, the electronically recorded image could be developed without expensive television studios. It was the most important step in Paik's incorporation of moving images, which are recorded in real time. The impact of this technology was profound. The clear act of recording images with the camera and watching them directly on the monitor gave immediate control over the image. Its portability allowed Paik to use it almost anywhere and the investment was low. Paik's technical knowledge, working with television and his real time experience of performance art, put him into a unique position for development of the artistic use of video.

As soon as Paik had bought the video tape recorder at the Liberty Music Shop in New York, he recorded his first video artwork called *Button Happening* at the store itself. The video showed the artist repeatedly buttoning and unbuttoning his coat. The new devices led him to other experiments, like just recording people awaiting the arrival of the Pope in New York in 1965, and were tested in various exhibitions like "Electronic Art II" at the Gallery Bonino, New York in 1968.

Dedicated to his strong experimental approach, Paik manipulated his recorded images by using powerful magnets, which he placed on top or the side of the television screen or through a self developed video synthesizer which offered him endless ways to alter the line patterns and colour of the electronic image. In 1968, Paik used that technology on an image of the philosopher Marshall McLuhan. At that time, McLuhan was playing a leading role as a media theory scientist. His major thesis that coined generations of scientists after him was the concept "The media is the message". He later developed the concept of the "Global Village" in a world with rapidly developing communication technique. These were a perfect fit to Paik's thoughts about video art. He was sure that the media itself was more important than the actual single piece or the content that was displayed in the produced films or video stills. In the McLuhan piece, Paik deformed through the use of a demagnetizer device an image of McLuhan so that it became a flittering unstable image. In that way, he gave appreciation to the great thinker.

In another television set artwork, called *Closed-circuit video installation*, Paik raised the question: what is life and reality? In the piece *Real Fish/Live Fish* (1982) the artist places two television monitors next to each other. On the left monitor (*Live Fish*) the television cathode was replaced and instead a tank with living fish was installed. To that monitor a video camera was connected, which captured the movements of the fish in the tank. This image was transferred to the second monitor (*Real Fish*) where the movements of the fish could be seen in real time. In *Real Plant/Live Plant* (1978) a television set was filled with earth and plants grew out of the top of the monitor. Embedded in the earth was a small monitor where the viewer could see the plants growing out of the television set.

In all "closed-circuit" pieces, Paik played with the question of reality, knowing the fundamental differences between Western culture, in which we take reality as what we see, and Eastern culture, in which reality is behind the observable objects of life.

Sculptures/Electronics

In installations like *Television Clock* (1963) and *Moon is the Oldest Television* (1965), Paik worked with large monitor sequences. In *Television Clock* 24 manipulated screens showed lines that appeared as clock pointers. These early installations became the blueprint for Paik's large video sculptures. A landmark installation was *Video Fish* (1975). This artwork was an installation of 20 monitors behind fish tank, which were lined in a row and positioned at eye level. Each of the monitors played edited videotapes showing different moving images. The images ranged from flying aeroplanes and fish to the famous New York choreographer and dancer Merce Cunningham dancing in a speeding collage of moving images. The viewer was confronted with a situation, whether he or she wanted to look at the monitors in order to look through the fish tank. This created a paradox; in the process of observation the fish tank became a television and the television a fish tank. Both perspectives seemed to constantly change their original purpose very much like in the *Real Fish/Live Fish* installation.

Paik achieved a remarkable dialogue through the fish tank and television images, by playing with the depth of the video space that he was able to change through the precise editing of videotapes. Again Paik played with the concept of time as a two-plane coordinate. Firstly, the stored and edited time of the videotape, secondly the unfolding and changing action of the fish. At random moments of the looped videotape a fish that was collaged into the video image emerged to fly or swim in its own space, which boosted the abstract dynamic of the installation. Through that manipulation, Paik was able to discontinue time and space of the installation and again confront the viewer with the question of what is real. The random interaction of Cunningham's choreography with the fish swimming in the tank created a dynamic dialogue of the movements and extended the video image itself. The question that comes to the viewers mind is: who is dancing with whom?

Paik's artistic way of working became very obvious here. Firstly, he put things together which do not relate to each other, secondly, he added more layers in order to make the situation more complex. But instead of changing and adjusting the different components to align them, Paik placed them side by side. He knew from his experience that the unadjusted situation could create meaning on a different and higher level. The artist was aware of this kind of thinking through his relation to Eastern Koan poetry. The Koan poetry techniques, as a way to guide a student to an enlightened mind, accept complexity as a given factor of life. Different from Western thinking which analyses the single parts of a situation in order to find a deductive answer, the answer in Eastern thinking comes to a person who is able to stand the complexity, in a particular moment.

Paik's work could be analysed in terms of the usage of materials and techniques, but it does not give an answer to most of his artworks, because of its complexity. They could only be understood through a longer process of perception. Paik knew the "mental technique", holding the observation in the mind, suspending rational thinking and waiting until an answer is given. It seems that he is saying to the viewer: look, it is not what you think, but through your own experience you might find an answer. This meta-concept counts for most of the later video sculptures which emerged sometimes as large video landscapes and where Paik pulled the viewer into the artwork itself.

In *Television Garden* plants of various sizes grew out of and around monitors lying with screens turned upside on the floor. Paik's famous videotape *Global Groove* (1973) was played in that installation. It was a groundbreaking video, a vision of the artist's dream of global television. The tape shifted between Paik's own synthesized imaginary production, video images of commercial television spots and parts of films of independent film makers. *Global Groove* played at the *Television Garden* reminded the viewer of McLuhan's idea of a global village growing together through the constant spread of television broadcast. In large scale pieces like *Fin de siècle II* (1989) and *Megatron/Matrix* (1995), Paik composed video imagery on a large scale with walls of monitors. These installations consisted of more than 200 monitors surrounded by *Jumbo Troms* that were a cluster of smaller television sets (approximately 40) and appeared like architectural environments. Sophisticated computer programmes allowed Paik to control the layers or amount of projected video films through which he worked against the consistency of the architectural structure of those installations, like in the huge 18 metre high Television tower *The More the Better* (1988) that he created for the Olympic games in Seoul. This artwork consisted of 1,003 monitors, was equipped with a three channel video projector and disintegrated space and time.

A Unique Position

The concept of disintegration by adding many layers of visuals reached a dramatic height in the video projection environment *Sistine Chapel* (1993) which Paik produced for the German Pavilion at the Venice Biennale. In this installation video projectors were arranged and combined in a way to create a vibrant and expressive display. On the surface of the ceilings and walls Paik collaged single projections into an overall image in order to create a dynamic visual space. As the viewer walked around the room and the projectors the entire space appeared to pulsate with the artist's moving images through the effect, the colours and the processed images of dancers. Abstract forms danced across the walls and overlapped each other in a free form, constantly changing a collage of great visual intensity. The whole room seemed to move as the projections eliminated the clear sense of space and, in that way, moved perception to an expanded level. In a technical way, Paik drew a line to the great spiritual European tradition.

In the original *Sistine Chapel* in Rome, Michelangelo created an overall painting structure for the first time that worked against the difficult architectural situation. Paik confronted the viewer with a situation where perception of reality became obsolete, through the complexity of overlaying forms, colours, patterns and images. Instead of "analysing" visual data the viewer had to accept the complexity of the installation as a matter of fact of a different form of reality.

If we look to the broad spectrum of Paik's work, there have been few artists who embodied in their thinking and creative approach a strong view of the possibilities of art. Paik is by all means a true utopian artist, searching constantly to find a better world for art. He reminds the viewer of the boundless genius of human spirit, equipped with a desire to cross the boundaries of science, technology, performance and music in order to expand the way that we make art and see the world in a new way. Through that the artist hits the core of art in the 20th Century itself: to stand the different and often inconsistent patterns of life and to adjust and transform these contradictions in order to create new meaning. Through Paik's positive vision of life and his use of subversive humour, he fostered the playful and fun aspect of his work providing new ways to imagine life as a *Global Groove*.

Conclusion

Looking at the impressive work of Paik and the way he was able to combine opposing ideas by juxtaposing them in order to envision and create new solutions, we see from the management perspective three major dimensions which might help executives to shape their organizations with the attitude of creation rather than simple managing. These dimensions are the way in which Paik was able to embrace and deal with complexity, the way he orchestrated the creativity of various people and ideas and the way he handled emotions to support his ideas.

Dealing with Complexity

The most important thing that Paik was able to do over and over again was to combine opposing ideas. He was able to combine the ideas of Eastern philosophy and Western technology, music and artistic performance, television and art, humans and machines, and technology and sexuality, just to name a few.

By doing so, Paik increased complexity. Only by increasing complexity through additional ideas and artistic perspectives, such as sound, video images and concepts of artist colleagues, who often came from different areas, was Paik able to develop new ideas and higher levels of artistic understanding. Looking at the way he was able to combine music and performance to create a new approach to art in his early work, two fundamental prerequisites for successfully combining ideas become obvious: mastery and dialogue. To deal with complexity efficiently one needs to have in-depth knowledge on the subject. Hence, when a conscious choice requires a certain perspective, or when what and how you observe in order to get relevant information is important, mastery helps to find such appropriate perspectives.

Paik had studied art history and history of music at the University of Tokyo. He had developed mastery in these two domains and continued to be a scholar in these fields when he moved to Europe. But mastery often creates the dilemma to develop a view that is too narrow. The expert often becomes blind to the most obvious alternative. Paik's open-minded attitude forced him into an ongoing internal dialogue between his two disciplines, art and music, to elicit new forms of combining the two in an innovative way. Also, the dialogue with his colleagues challenged and broadened his way of making art.

Looking at modern organizations, we therefore propose that managers when engaging in product or process innovation or designing new business models have to rethink their approach towards complexity, embracing it rather than reducing it. Most organizations call for the reduction of complexity. The challenge is to find the right proportion of complexity to answer the various demands of the market and to face competition. An example for defining the "right" grade of complexity is the high tec scale company Toledo. Some years ago the company faced a typical copy–paste problem. Asian competitors were able to enter the market with a copied model half a year after the launch of a new version. Toledo addressed that problem and decided to increase complexity dramatically. The company built mechanical inaccuracies into the scales purposely and adjusted them using sophisticated software.

By defining the appropriate complexity, services managers can jump to the next level by giving their products and solutions a new meaning. To do so companies first of all have to master their own field, which means not only mastering technology and processes to produce and sell products but also mastering the overall customer experience. In addition to that, managers should engage in a dialogue with all relevant stakeholders.

For example, Apple has been able to re-invent itself by combining opposing ideas and markets over and over again. Apple had a long tradition in the PC market, having pioneered the first usable personal computing devices in the late 1980s. It stood for ease of use, a proprietary operating system, strong brand and industrial design. In 2001 Apple shifted to the "digital hub" strategy combining different markets like entertainment, software, PC, video games and telephony just to name a few. The shift was initiated by the debut of the iPod in 2001, the iTunes music store in 2003, followed by the iPhone in 2007 and the iPad in 2010. These new products put Apple on the path to becoming a fully-fledged digital convergence company. The change in the company's name from Apple Computer Inc to Apple Inc in 2007 marked the official repositioning of the company. While today, this strategic move seems all too logical and is supported by the technological convergence taking place, it was a bold decision at the time, trying to combine technological shifts. For example, the advances in gaming devices which allowed customers to watch DVDs and go online, smart phones that increasingly functioned as handheld computers and, last but not least, changes in customer experience. Apple could have chosen to stay in the PC industry as many of its rivals did and optimized their established performance criteria. But instead they invested heavily in better understanding their customer by interacting with their customers, but more so their non-customers, to develop the appropriate business model for the music player industry. They understood that they would only succeed with a complete system that combines hardware, software, services and content. In addition to that they had to innovate at high speed and cover all the price points, contrary to their strategy in the PC business where they only offered premium pricing. Their deep market understanding and the in-depth dialogue with their customers and potential customers enabled them to successfully combine seemingly opposing strategies and markets.

For managers, it means that in the early stages of innovation they should resist simplifying and contrasting, and instead engage in open and constructive dialogue. In order to do that, executives have to find new formats for bringing ideas together in an atmosphere of trust and respect. It is important to look for patterns, connections and causal relations instead of simply doing what they have done successfully in the past.

Orchestrating Creativity

A second element in Paik's approach to innovation in the field of art is his way of orchestrating creativity. Through his close collaboration with musicians, artists and scientists like Karl-Heinz Stockhausen, John Cage, Charlotte Moorman and Josef Beuys, just to name a few, he was able to tap into deep sources of inspiration for his work. Especially by collaborating with Moorman, Paik was able to progress in a way he would not have been able to on his own. He could push his interest in music and performance into fields like sexuality, partnership and the role of people, especially women, in music. With all his collaborators he shared the belief that they could advance through a transdisciplinary approach and often they had a shared vision of where and how far to go. The collaboration was project based, with a clear beginning and a clear ending, and was very remarkable in the art world at that time. Up to that point Western artists were often sort of "lone geniuses". Paik stepped on virgin soil with his way of producing art on a collaboration level. The characteristic feature of his way of working is the difference between conducting and orchestrating creativity. As a conductor of an orchestra you lead the interpretation of the music being played from your perspective. There is not much room for creativity for the single player. Orchestrating creativity is more the work of a composer thinking what kind of instrument he needs for a specific piece of music to create the appropriate sound. Taking this idea there is practical impact mostly in a chamber orchestra. There is no real leader (maybe an informal one) and the quality of the music played emerges from the ability to listen to each other and to respond quickly at the same time. The aim of that understanding of such playing is to create a "sounding body", a quality that is possible for a listener to experience immediately. Paik was constantly searching for that level of interaction in his work with colleagues, being and not being a leader at the same time. His Eastern background, to step back to see the greater idea, might have helped him to develop such a characteristic of collective creativity.

For managers this means that it is important to actively think about ways to orchestrate for creativity, within the company or even outside of the company. In both cases managers have to identify and test shared beliefs, values and visions, define the project clearly and find the appropriate business model for the venture.

Think of IBM in the early 1990s, when the company successfully transformed itself. One important element in this transformation was the decision to look outside the company for new ideas and to actively orchestrate creativity. While the company had practically invented the computer industry and had created inside its own labs the core technologies in hardware and software, IBM was forced in the early 1990s to turn to external technologies. For example, IBM did not come up with software in the company's lab for the Internet. But, in order to do so, they had to open up and actively seek cooperation with suppliers and, even more importantly, customers. In the process, IBM set up a programme called First of a Kind (FOAK) in which IBM and a key customer would jointly work on a commercially important and, from the research point of view, challenging problem. A dedicated research team from IBM worked for a pre-defined period at the customer site together with a dedicated team from the customer side. IBM was able to get its hands on real time data in a controlled environment while the customer got their problem fixed. Furthermore, IBM was exposing its research staff to the current issues of its main customers and also the right to use that solution later on for other customers. However, this meant that IBM also had to change other parts of its up to then predominant business model. For example, the role of the researcher changed from a pure knowledge generator to a knowledge broker, inside the company between the business group and the research division as well as outside the company towards the customer. The kind of researchers that IBM was looking for would also change. Presently IBM is also trying to identify their ability to work with customers and generate solutions to their problems and, last but not least, the role of the manager from the business group also changed as more knowledge about the various activities within the research organization was generated, which would enable him or her to better link the outputs of the labs with the needs of the customers.

For managers this meant that they had to focus on identifying and testing shared beliefs, values and vision, clearly define the project scope and find the appropriate business model for the venture.

Emotionalizing

The last element of Paik's ability to hold opposing positions in mind in order to envision and to create new solutions was his way of emotionalizing his ideas. This was always one of the core functions of art. Think of a traditional artwork like the famous stuccowork *The Creation of Adam* by Michelangelo on the ceiling of the Sistine Chapel in Rome. Besides the mythological story and its "actors" (God and Adam) the artwork shows a warm and fatherly power of God being close to humans (nearly touching them). Through this radical interpretation (the closeness of God to humans) Michelangelo underlined the emotional redefinition of the image of God that met very closely the new understanding of religion at the Renaissance time. The artist changed the image of God from a distant figure to someone who embraces humans with generosity.

Paik's emotionalization was the unique humour he brought into performance art, installation and video sculpture. His source was the close relationship to the Fluxus group he belonged to from the beginning and his sympathy for Dada art. The Dada approach, with its tendency for experimental settings, the conscious choice to combine non-related things intuitively and often create nonsense as active provocation, opened a world for Paik that respected his cultural and artistic background and let him create his own story. Paik did not have to become a European artist – he simply used the different art formats (as juxtapositions) and created unexpected new forms that were often very humorous. *Zen for Head*, Paik performing as a cello in the cooperation with Moorman in a John Cage composition, the construction of the early *Robot K-456* and later the series family of robots, all these pieces showed an incredible ability to use humour as an artistic tactic to get his message across. Paik's aim was to question the development and the consumer side of modern technology, letting the viewer sit back often in an unsure situation. Talking about emotions as drivers, Paik stepped into the role of a modern zany in order to mirror the ongoing change of technology and its impact on daily life.

The Paik example implies for managers in modern organizations, that they have to develop the ability to work with emotions, often through the appropriate images. Managers have to understand the emotional potential of the organization and where these emotions are anchored. Therefore, it is important to know the roots, traditions, stories and powerful images that the company culture is built upon. Managers have to be familiar with the actual heartbeat of the organization and emotional demands of the employees, the customers and other stakeholders. Managing emotions implies that the manager has to know the important stories from the past in order to re-invent the vision and change the direction of the company through a new storyline using sustainable, emotional images. One of the core questions of managers who intend to create new solutions is: how can I convince the customers, but also my own organization, my employees and stakeholders of these new solutions? The challenge is to create an emotional container for the new ideas and solutions. So, managers have to develop the right stories, find the appropriate images and create a dramaturgy in order to give the new ideas a face, convince customers, align people and move the organization forward.

Think of Daimler's attempt to emotionalize its communication to support its vision of a sustainable organization. The claim of the new campaign, launched officially through a commercial in June 2010, is: "The best or nothing". The film starts with a sequence of the founder Gottlieb Daimler sitting on a construction desk with closed eyes, envisioning the future. He falls asleep. "Every great story has its beginning: The dream to build the first automobile and to invent it again and again" is the opener. The film shows milestones of the Mercedes Benz history (the silver arrow race car), the cars people never forget (the wing car from the 1970s) and technological leadership for the future (fuel cell and e-cars). Then a voice interrupts that dream and the film goes back to Gottlieb Daimler. "Mr. Daimler (he awakes) you are working too much", says a simple cleaning woman. "Are you sure?" he asks, "But I just want the best, simply the best."

Mercedes-Benz started that brand message first as part of the company vision/mission guidelines at the end of 2009 addressing employees and stakeholders. It was very controversial. On one side the claim and the story found positive resonance amongst its employees, as the message underlines traditional values like perfection, quality and fascination and combines it with future values like responsibility for ecological environment and sustainability. On the other side, the message is still rather broad and customers and employees were uncertain about the actual meaning of "The best or nothing". Is it the best technology (from an engineering perspective), the best low cost production (from a controlling perspective) or is it just the best brand (from a marketing perspective). This of course shows the delicate balance managers have to strike when using emotions to support new solutions and ideas.

The challenge for managers actively working with emotions is that they and their statements are immediately put to the test (does he walk the talk?). It is an effective but also risky way to work within an organization. Employee's sense immediately if the story a manager creates, the images used, the tradition referred to has a meaning for that manager or not. All these ingredients must be true to the teller.

Mastering the three dimensions dealing with complexity, orchestrating creativity and handling emotions has the potential to turn management into the art of leadership.

Additional Literature

Atwater, J.B., Kannan, V.R. and Stephens, A.A. (2008) Cultivating Systemic Thinking in the Next Generation of Business Leaders, *Academy of Management Learning & Education*, **7**(1): 9–25.

Cao, G., Clarke, S. and Lehaney, B. (1999) Towards systemic management of diversity in organizational change, *Strategic Change*, **8**: 205–216.

Carucci, R. (2006) Building Relationships that enable next-generation leaders, *Leader to Leader Journal – Executive Forum*, **Fall**(42): 47–53.

Deutsche Guggenheim (2004) *Global Groove*, exhibition.

Goleman, D. (2007) *Social Intelligence: The New Science of Human Relationship*, New York: Random House.

Hanhardt, J.G. (2000) *The world of Nam June Paik*, exhibition catalogue Guggenheim Museum.

Kanter, R.M. (2003) Leadership and the Psychology of Turnarounds, *Harvard Business Review*, **81**(6 June): 58–67.

Kohlrieser, G. (2006) The Power of Authentic Dialogue, *Leader to Leader Journal*, **Fall**(42): 36–40.

Neuburger, S., Ammer, M. and Schmidt, T. (2009) *Nam June Paik: Exposition of Music, Electronic Television, Revisited*, Berlin: Buchhandlung Walther Konig GmbH & Co. KG. Abt. Verlag.

Richardson, K.A. (2008) Managing Complex Organizations: Complexity Thinking and the Science and Art of Management, *E:CO*, **10**(2): 13–26.

Stockhausen, K. (1964) *Texte zu eigenen Werken, Zur Kunst Anderer, Actuelles, Aufsätze 1952–1962 zur musikalischen Praxis*, exhibition catalogue, Cologne, reprint, Paik video, p. 29.

van Gerstner, L. (2003) *Who Says Elephants Can't Dance?: Leading a Great Enterprise through Dramatic Change*, London: Harper Business.

CHAPTER 8

Interview with Gerrit Gohlke, artnet

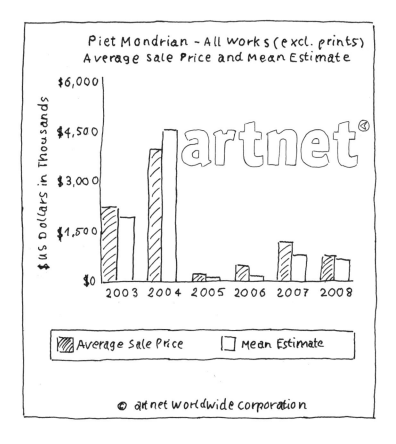

Piet Mondrian - All works (excl. prints)
Average Sale Price and Mean Estimate

Average Sale Price   Mean Estimate

© artnet worldwide corporation

Introduction

In the summer of 2010 we had several meetings with Gerrit Gohlke, the editor in chief of artnet magazine to discuss global trends and underlying currents of the art market. We discussed whether companies are artists or gallerists or both and what it is that companies can learn from the arts.

artnet was founded 1998 in Germany and is today the place to buy, sell and research fine art online. They have the largest online Gallery Network with over 2,200 galleries in more than 250 cities worldwide, more than 166,000 artworks by over 39,000 artists from around the globe. The Network serves dealers and art buyers alike by providing a survey of the market and its pricing trends, as well as the means to communicate instantly, inexpensively and globally. One key servies is artnet Magazine, the insider's guide to the art market with daily news, reviews, and features by renowned writers in the art community and the Price Database. artnet's Price Database is a comperhensive archive of the fine art auction results worldwide. Representing auction results from over 500 international auction houses since 1985, the Price Database covers more than 4 million auction results by over 188,000 artists, ranging from Old Masters to Cotemporary Art.

Reckhenrich: Is there a major new trend on the art market?

Gohlke: It is hard to say what is considered a trend and what people take seriously as a trend. There are trends on the art market which only influence that market. Prices rise and fall; movements are similar to those on the stock markets. What we currently have is a situation more like speculation, however. Art historians of the future will find it hard to understand today's fashions.

Kupp: 2010 saw the art business shaken by a severe recession. Some believe the new trend is a return to serious subjects.

Gohlke: Art still draws its credibility from the history of art. Everyone acts as if each work were part of a canon of everlasting value; that is why crises shake the art market worse than the steel industry. Dealers and collectors are afraid the market will lose its bearings if suddenly confronted with its own transience which is why, in the wake of a crisis, people look for works which are not simply aimed at bringing in a high price. Enduring worth is sought in place of mere status. That is on the one hand a sign of real hope for less haste – in times of crisis, even the market realizes that good new art is not produced overnight. On the other hand, proclaiming true, honest values is invariably also a blatant marketing ruse for the benefit of the collectors, for what buyer would happily invest millions in works which tomorrow turn out to be part of a passing fad? Even if the art world has always produced passing fads which are now gathering dust in museum storage rooms . . .

Reckhenrich: You mean to say that artistic depth is just one of many trends?

Gohlke: I am a critic and find depth a great product; however there are now as many trends as there are artists. Like any other culture market, the art business continues to produce both stars and also-rans, revolutionary innovation and complete banality. There is no universally applicable criterion for good art, which is why collectors have instead long placed their trust in works which are simply expensive. Yet such a lack of discrimination brings its own punishment when prices fall in a crisis. Well-informed collectors are therefore now focussing more on art which has a recognizable context. If that is a trend, it certainly cannot be defined in terms of historic style. Collectors must take their own decision on whom to trust and that is why they now have such a great opportunity to discover and promote; to look for and follow the ideas of tomorrow. Without strategy or faith in ideas, no players on the market will produce anything but expensive rubbish – and that goes for collectors, artists and dealers alike.

Kupp: Are there various response strategies open to artists on this complex market; a range of business models for artists, so to speak?

Gohlke: The art market has grown exponentially. At the top end, it merges with other creative industries and adopts their rules. It is not a simple, easy to understand market but a highly segmented one. Here too, as on the music or film market, there are the carefully calculated (and often formulaic) major blockbusters which only succeed thanks to the concerted efforts of dealers. And of course there are also investors looking for high returns. There is also a parallel independent market on which innovative new artists can establish themselves more quickly, where the budgets are low, where some work is even produced for the insider and where good old artistic expertise still means something. Good art develops slowly and artists' careers cannot be forecast in business plans; that is why work often evolves on this market which years later turns out to be the real capital in major collections. There is also an almost impenetrable market which tends to challenge trends and faith in trends. A market on which the outsider can find perfect innovations and new developments away from the cameras of the glamour magazines. This is where artists' art for the initiated is born. Those who take the trouble to penetrate this market will discover many of the trends of tomorrow.

Kupp: So trying to find the one and only major new trend is a lost cause from the outset?

Gohlke: These segments in the art market exist in parallel and are unconnected, yet collectors, buyers and critics still have a habit of talking about "the art market". This is a reflection of the pathetic belief, or let us say the romantic hope, that art exists in one great overarching tradition covering everything that is of worth and quality from Leonardo to today, from mediaeval frescoes to the work of Jeff Koons. That the greatest genius will win in the end and his art be proved a priceless treasure. In fact, the reality on the art market is one of passing trends and ever more transient effects, of hyped names and of skyrocketing prices. That is what is so great about the market – only afterwards can you see what developments are truly sustainable and what may just have been a bubble.

Reckhenrich: Yet one single work of art can cost millions. Buyers pay astronomical prices at which the general public can only marvel. Some prospective buyers are apparently agreed on what is more valuable than everything else.

Gohlke: Art critics such as Wolfgang Ullrich have suggested there is such a lack of orientation on the art market that only the price itself can be taken as a fixed quality criterion. What Ullrich describes is fundamentally a growing obsession with the expensive which has resulted in rare older works valued for centuries often being cheaper than spectacular new ones. A classic example is Damien Hirst, at best a middle-of-the-road artist, who plays on this fascination with price and has made it the real object of his art. The "golden calf" he sold at a spectacular Sotheby's auction in 2008 is the ultimate expression of this approach. Expensive materials and big gestures have turned Hirst's works into luxury items. Critics, collectors and dealers have been protesting ever since about the fact that this art is so expensive. Being more expensive than everyone or everything else has become a sign of artistic uniqueness in an era of reproduction in which precious little else is unique.

Reckhenrich: But don't all investments in such art secure a long-term interest in it?

Gohlke: A look at the Museum of Decorative Arts in Berlin is proof that glittering, sparkling wonders of the world do not necessarily guarantee later artistic appreciation. The museum contains a host of mechanical marvels which left their princely commissioners under mounds of debt or even bankrupt. Where are the artists who have been seriously influenced by Hirst? There were also once a well-known group of artists called "Neue Wilde" who earned magnificent country homes and enjoyed ostentatious luxury in the 1980s

with their neoexpressionist paintings. None now know better than their collectors how meaningless this art has become at an international level. Each
day probably sees another work from this school disappear into storage.
Works by the odd strict conceptualist or the odd radical contextual artist from
the same period are now of greater value. So what is value? Value is work
which shows development, work which has room to breathe rather than
hyperventilating at an art show in Miami for a few years.

Kupp: But not even room to breathe will help if no one invests.

Gohlke: That is a question of interest and speed. There are single-minded and
   unwavering collectors, and the most successful are often those who follow
   artists over the years, pay attention to them and therefore ultimately often
   collect the better works – frequently over decades, during which time the
   art gradually becomes established on the market with gradually increasing
   prices. No serious critic, dealer, expert or curator would say Maria Lassnig
   is a less important artist than Damien Hirst simply because it took her
   years to achieve high prices on the secondary market, in other work art
   dealerships and auction houses. Part of the crisis on the art market we
   have just experienced was caused by an obsession with auction prices.
   People at the top end of the market were investing in an inflationary machine. Price pressure made the expensive even more expensive and led to
   this art alone being constantly over-valued, something common enough in
   such a fast-paced trade.

Reckhenrich: What do you have against high prices?

Gohlke: High prices mean printing money instead of innovating. That is why
   smarter gallery owners have tried to prevent their artists becoming part of
   this inflationary system. They want to see collections showing art which
   gives their artists credibility. A collector should not simply buy; he should
   also be able to vouch for the quality of what he owns. Those who buy on
   speculation and rapidly resell will soon be shown the door by intelligent
   galleries. So I have nothing against high prices. But the fact that the classic
   works we admire in museums are now expensive should not lead us to con-
   clude that the modern works which are expensive now will be admired in
   museums forever. Criteria for innovative, influential ideas are not necessarily identical to those for blockbuster successes and that is as true in the
   art business as in the film industry.

Kupp: What are the criteria for success on the so-called blockbuster market?

Gohlke: Recognition value and good PR. Let's stay with Damien Hirst, who I
   believe also appears in your book. Hirst had excellent advisors and a superb

manager in the person of Frank Dunphy, who to all intents and purposes took on the role of producer. Hirst did of course also have powerful sponsors and became a model artist on a London market which was hungry for sensation. But Hirst's creation of the diamond skull, an artwork so expensive it was only bought by a consortium of bidders to which the artist himself belonged; the fact that the prices continued to rise and the artist therefore proceeded to bypass his own galleries and flog everything left at auction – that is a game of business poker of the first order. It has little to do with intelligent art unless the poker game itself becomes art. It merely demonstrates that what we once called art has now fragmented into a number of different markets. Hirst's market is a highly expensive media business . . .

Reckhenrich: . . . in which Hirst is a successful super-star.

Gohlke: In this business, he is a winner. This is a business which tells artists' and collectors' home stories and transforms art into a media saga for the tabloid press. Consortia are who ultimately profit from the global brand this creates. In the business of artistic innovation, however, Hirst is a loser. His latest rather banal paintings which are no longer the work of assistants but of the "master" himself are currently being trashed in the British papers. Superstars are the product of networks. The art history network may however differ from that of the current gallery and auction business.

Reckhenrich: Is the blockbuster market easier to manipulate than others?

Gohlke: If one considers that an influential gallery owner can now become curator of a museum in Los Angeles without such role switching producing any outcry in the art world, artistic quality would appear to be an elastic term. A former market player and his museum board will determine the success of artists in whose work he may once have invested. The art world still sees itself as a separate universe with its own rules. Supervisory bodies which sanction abuse are yet to appear. Yet the more populist the major museums are, the easier it will be to promote artists who are successful above all as brands because they constantly repeat themselves and their stories are particularly good. The art business has its own Britney Spears and its own Robbie Williams. That is not necessarily the art I believe will still be dominating museums and major private collections in 20 or 30 years.

Reckhenrich: Yet art is not a scientific creation. Even Hirst is not a synthetic construct. Creativity is still a major part of art. From Fluxus to the Impressionists, there have been many artists and artwork which were the products of single ideas and yet shape our understanding of art today – including our understanding of objective value. Can companies learn

*creativity from art and the art market if they do not allow themselves to be
hypnotized by prices and hype?*

Gohlke: That would depend entirely on what business wants to learn. You
could learn that mindlessly pursuing one single course, for example creating a sculpture by arranging railway sleepers on the ground and subsequently continuing to arrange railway sleepers and call it sculpture, can
be enormously successful. You see that again and again; even the least
informed observer in a populist exhibition aiming to draw visitors in their
millions will realize that the railway sleepers on the floor are the work of
Carl Andre. That is in a way general knowledge and it would be much
harder if the artist had completely new, entirely different phases of work
over the years in cyclical, creative waves.

Kupp: That is then the brand identity.

Gohlke: Precisely. Now, there are artists who do produce cyclical innovations
and radical new developments but whose personal style nevertheless remains
clearly recognisable. That is what makes Picasso the phenomenon everyone
thinks of when asked about the greatest works of the *Avant-garde* movement.
Who is the first artist to occur to people when you ask them about art? Picasso,
or possibly van Gogh. People do not necessarily think of Nam June Paik or
Piero Manzoni. If you ask them to name the most important minimalists, they
will think of Donald Judd and Carl Andre and not of Jo Baer, the intellectual
pioneer of Minimalism who constantly called herself and the entire artistic
movement into question. The reason is simple. Baer not only painted the clev-
erest Minimalist pictures which clearly, brilliantly and beautifully reflect the
entire theoretical discussion on the objectivity of images. She also ultimately
announced that she had exhausted the intellectual scope of serial repetition
and, at the height of her fame, switched genres. To the horror of critics and
collectors, she then devoted herself to Figuration.

Kupp: The end of a promising brand . . .

Gohlke: Fortunately, wouldn't you agree? At first, no one would talk to the artist
any more. She lived in Ireland and focussed all her creativity on new issues.
This led to the gradual emergence of an extremely interesting new *oeuvre*
which now appears in many ways younger and more experimental than the
paintings of contemporary artists 50 years her junior. Some day the museums
will also catch up on this development and "discover" the work they previously ignored. That is exactly what happened with Louise Bourgeois.

*Kupp: A difficult concept for a company to swallow – waiting decades for suc-
cess is not a particularly attractive model . . .*

Gohlke: I knew you wouldn't like my example. In this case, there were even problems keeping the work on the market at all. There was time when galleries were positively embarrassed about showing Baer's work – completely untrendy and worlds away from what people had once liked about her. Yet Baer's story is a lesson in determination, and possibly also in a certain decisiveness which means moving on from past achievements.

Reckhenrich: The ability to learn is an extremely interesting aspect for an organization as it needs to remember and learn from company history . . .

Gohlke: The business world would be well off if companies were as capable of learning as Jo Baer. Jeff Koons would be a better prospect for an investor as his work has always paid off in hard cash for collectors. If the odd critic would nevertheless prefer Baer to Koons on his or her living room wall, the question is what that should teach us. Conformity or to question trends?

Reckhenrich: But what is the secret to Baer's creativity? How has she managed to keep developing new works over all these years?

Gohlke: Contrariness? A joy in new discoveries? Baer decided to concentrate on something new after her first retrospective. She believed the initial problem was more or less resolved and she could now look for new problems. The radicalism and unconcern which mean not asking what to do in order to satisfy others but instead asking oneself "What must I do so I can respond to the next major question in my field?" has always seemed to me to be an admirable approach. Couldn't Gottlieb Daimler have become a Baer collector? To sacrifice as rapid as possible a new success for a lasting development which is slow but unaffected by trends is a fascinating decision. Art cannot teach companies how to make a quick buck. What it can teach them is where to find creativity. Namely in wilful unconcern.

Kupp: Could one also say the market ought to have revised its opinion of Jo Baer sooner?

Gohlke: As we have seen, there is a lot to be learned from the art market including just how stupid the market can be. The market took a long time to understand that an artist was going through several stages of development and that the end result was an extremely interesting oevre. Those who only look at prices and see art as a share investment with added glamour will certainly still fail to understand her work. There is no standard rule for the market. There have been no sharp breaks in the work of Bruce Nauman, yet he is an extremely innovative and talented artist who has honed his work epoch for epoch. A good investment and also a breathtakingly fascinating oevre. If one were to compare Nauman and Baer and ask what distinguishes out from artists who slavishly follow the market trends and produce the tedious and banal, it would be their unwavering search for insight. Companies could learn to value Nauman and to appreciate and support Baer.

Kupp: Nauman's potential was easier to use.

Gohlke: He also had the right galleries. However, it's true enough that there are all sorts of people on the art market, only a few of whom would also be successful in the used car or insurance business. True, this market like others has its consummate self-promoters. Yet the self-promoter in art does not always keep the promises he makes. At least as interesting are the explorative artists, who are often late developers. Nam June Paik is an explorative type, a developer like the nerds in the IT sector. One who at first just sits there and plays around with a new technology before considering what exactly it could produce. You can never take the success of one type to mean another type is worth less. A painter like Hodler, who produced x variations on the same lake scene simply to earn his bread, deepened the nuances in his painting with each variation and, strangely enough, painted a good picture almost every time, with almost every repetition. The question is always this: can I come back from this approach to my original aim as an artist? At the heart of this question is invariably a desire for exploration or the search for clear and immediate insight.

Reckhenrich: But what can one manager learn from this diversity? The knowledge that success has many forms and creativity many different facets is in itself nothing new.

Gohlke: What fascinates me first and foremost is whether the manager should learn from the artist or from the gallery owner. When you talk about innovation, it seems to me unclear whether the manager is really to be the artist and innovator or indeed the one who must recognize and understand the innovations. Perhaps, after all, the manager should have more of the gallery owner about him. Many great gallery owners are successful in the long term because they allow changes and learn how to make them. That is not an easy job. Imagine an artist changes course every few years. The gallery owner visits the studio to find with mild surprise or indeed a severe sense of shock something very different from that which he has been so successfully selling to collectors for the last two years. What should he say to the artist now? If you look at good gallery owners when they visit studios, the way they deal with the artists, the way they support such works, the first thing you will notice is the passion with which they are prepared to tell their artists' stories instead of going off and forcing their artists to repeat and copy themselves. I believe that innovation on the art market is also dependent upon this interaction between a good gallery owner, who truly thinks for the long term, and a good artist who shares his experience with this gallery owner. Rather than buying the art business' cheesy myths of the genius at work, a company could perhaps learn far more from this interaction than from individual artistic achievements which, after a few years in a museum, look as if they had appeared from nowhere.

Reckhenrich: The company would in that case be both artist and gallery owner . . .

Gohlke: Yes, and somewhere in this constellation there are also the collectors. Including those one can only respect and marvel at: collectors who happily ignore the course the gallery market wants them to follow and keep on collecting new work and supporting and believing in young artists. Some collectors have had a greater influence on the history of art than certain populist museum curators. Works are bought, exchanged, revised . . . and also occasionally sold. Such a portfolio is driven by a motivation very different from the promise of high prices, even if the steady rise in value which such collections usually experience in the long term is a pleasant reward.

Kupp: You believe the art market rewards self-confidence, indeed perhaps even obstinacy?

Gohlke: It certainly rewards self-assurance. What I find the most exciting on the art market is the radicalness and courage to trust in one's own subjective judgement. Not to say "where is conformist pressure taking us today?", but rather "I know that what I am looking at is interesting; I could be mistaken but I am willing to take that risk". That is a quality which characterizes all three: the dealer in the middle, the artist on one hand and the intelligent collector collecting for the long term on the other. The ultimate aim is, incidentally, pleasure. Pleasure in being radical and not doing today what you did yesterday.

Reckhenrich: The art market is a complex one with a wide range of players. What is the role of artnet and what could companies learn from artnet?

Gohlke: That success can come from not depending on myths. That market transparency is beneficial to sellers and buyers alike. Before the advent of artnet, it was hard for buyers to negotiate a fair price on the art market. artnet has shed light on the business, light of which the informed collector was in urgent need in order to finance daring innovations and quality. When buyer and seller now meet at an exhibition, it can be assumed that each has already checked the price database and gallery network for information on potential prices and has read our art magazines to find out what critics think of a particular artist. Equality has replaced mystery. That creates trust on the market and helps combat exaggeration. People can learn from us that conventions and traditions can be changed. When Hans Neuendorf laid the foundations for the current database business with his visionary price data collection, the predictions were that he would fail. The conservative art market, so went the argument, relied on individual business relationships. Yet the fact that buyers and sellers are now equally well-informed has in fact boosted market players' long-term turnover. The blind purchase of art is of as little benefit as uninformed investments on the property market. Collectors can now have more confidence in their own decisions because artnet has cleared away the myths and legends. That is the best thing for art that could have happened – and the fact that the odd objective criterion could be good for a market has now been recognized by many people even in the field of investment banking.

Reckhenrich: Many thanks for talking to us, Mr Gohlke.

Additional Literature

Crow, K. (2008) The Man Behind Damien Hirst – Frank Dunphy has helped make the artist a fortune, *The Wall Street Journal*, Sunday 7 September 2008, http://online.wsj.com/article/SB122066050737405813.html

O'Hagan, S. (2007) The man who sold us Damien, *The Observer*, Sunday 1 July 2007, http://www.guardian.co.uk/artanddesign/2007/jul/01/art1

Ullrich, W. (2009) Art, Price & Value—Über den Wert der Kunst, *artnet Magazin*, 28 February, http://www.artnet.de/magazine/art-price-value-uber-den-wert-der-kunst-teil-i/

REFERENCES

Abell, D. (1980) *Defining the Business: The Starting Point of Strategic Planning*, Englewood Cliffs, NJ: Prentice-Hall Inc.

Amabile, T.M., Conti, R., Coon, H., Lazenby, J. and Herron, M. (1996) Assessing the work environment for creativity, *Academy of Management Journal*, **39**(5 October): 1154–1184.

Amabile, T.M. and Khaire, M. (2008) Creativity and the role of the leader, *Harvard Business Review*, October, 10: 100–109.

Anderson, J. and Kupp, M. (2006) Madonna: Entrepreneurship on a Dance Floor, *Business Strategy Review*, **17**(4): 26–31.

Anderson, J. and Kupp, M. (2006) Retail Financial Services in Germany, *ESMT Case Study*.

Anderson, J. and Kupp, M. (2008) MLP AG, *ESMT Case Study*.

Anderson, J. and Kupp, M. (2008) Virgin Mobile UK, *ESMT-TiasNimbas Case Study*.

Atwater, J.B., Kannan, V.R. and Stephens, A.A. (2008) Cultivating Systemic Thinking in the Next Generation of Business Leaders, *Academy of Management Learning & Education*, **7**(1): 9–25.

Bakker, N. and Jansen, L. (2010) *The Real van Gogh: The Artist and His Letters*, London: Thames & Hudson.

Barling, J., Weber, T. and Kelloway, E.K. (1996) Effects of transformational leadership training on attitudinal and financial outcomes: A field experiment, *Journal of Applied Psychology*, **81**: 827–832.

Barnes, E. (2003) What's your story? *Harvard Management Communication Letter*, 3–5 July.

Bass, B.M., Avolio, B.J. and Goodheim, L. (1987) Biography and the Assessment of Transformational Leadership at the World-Class Level, *Journal of Management*, **13**: 7–19.

Brown, T. (2008) Design Thinking, *Harvard Business Review*, **92**(June): 85–92.

Cao, G., Clarke, S. and Lehaney, B. (1999) Towards systemic management of diversity in organizational change, *Strategic Change*, **8**: 205–216.

Carucci, R. (2006) Building Relationships that enable next-generation leaders, *Leader to Leader Journal – Executive Forum*, **Fall**(42): 47–53.

Catmull, E. (2008) How Pixar Fosters Collective Creativity, *Harvard Business Review*, **86**(9 September): 64–72.

Charitou, C. and Markides, C. (2003) Responses to Disruptive Strategic Innovation, *Sloan Management Review*, **44**(2 Winter): 55–63.

Conger, J.A. (1998) The Necessary Art of Persuasion, *Harvard Business Review*, May–June: 85–95.

Crow, K. (2008) The Man Behind Damien Hirst – Frank Dunphy has helped make the artist a fortune, *The Wall Street Journal*, Sunday 7 September 2008, http://online.wsj.com/article/SB122066050737405813.html

Deutsche Guggenheim (2004) *Global Groove*, exhibition.

Dobni, C.B. (2010) Achieving synergy between strategy and innovation: The key to value creation, *International Journal of Business Science & Applied Management*, **5** (1 January): 48–58.

Eagly, A.H. (2003) The rise of female leaders, *Zeitschrift für Sozialpsychologie*, **34**: 123–132. http://www.forbes.com/lists/2009/53/celebrity-09_The-Celebrity-100_Rank.html

Friedman, T. (2006) *The World is Flat: A brief history of the globalized world in the twenty-first century*, New York: Penguin Books Ltd.

Fuller, J.B., Patterson, C.E.P., Hester, K. and Stringer, S.Y. (1996) A quantitative review of research on charismatic leadership, *Psychological Reports*, **78**: 271–287.

Gardner, H. (1995) *Leading Minds: An Anatomy of Leadership*, New York: Basic Books.

Gauguin, P., Guerin, D. and Levieux, E. (1996) *Writings of a Savage PB: Paul Gauguin*, Da Capo Press.

Goleman, D. (2007) *Social Intelligence: The New Science of Human Relationship*, New York: Random House.

Grant, R.M. (2002) *Contemporary Strategy Analysis: Concepts, Techniques and Applications*, Oxford: Blackwell Publishers Inc.

Guber, P. (2007) The Four Truths of the Storyteller, *Harvard Business Review*, December: 53–59.

Hall, G. (2008) Inside the theory of U, *Reflections*, **9**(1): 41–46.

Hanhardt, J.G. (2000) *The world of Nam June Paik*, exhibition catalogue Guggenheim Museum.

Harlan, V. (2010) *Was ist Kunst?*, Urachhaus, Auflage; 6. A.

Hetzer, T. (1969) *Tizian Geschichte seiner Farbe*, Frankfurt am Main: Vittorio Klostermann Verlag.

House, R.J., Spangler, W.D. and Woycke, J. (1991) Personality and Charisma in the United-States Presidency – A Psychological Theory of Leader Effectiveness, *Administrative Science Quarterly*, **36**: 364–396.

Hughes, R. (2004) That's show business, *The Guardian*, 30 June 2004.

Hughes, R. (2008) Day of the Dead, *The Guardian*, 13 December 2008.

Kanter, R.M. (2003) Leadership and the Psychology of Turnarounds, *Harvard Business Review*, **81**(6 June): 58–67.

Kim, C. and Mauborgne, R. (1997) Value Innovation: The Strategic Logic of High Growth, *Harvard Business Review*, January–February: 103–112.

Kim, W.C. and Mauborgne, R. (1999) Creating New Market Space, *Harvard Business Review*, January–February: 83–93.

Kohlrieser, G. (2006) The Power of Authentic Dialogue, *Leader to Leader Journal*, **Fall**(42): 36–40.

Kupp, M. and Anderson, J. (2009) *Celtel Nigeria, ESMT Case Study: Case A and Case B*, ESMT-309-00(96/97)-1.

Kupp, M., Anderson, J. and Moaligou, R. (2009) Lessons from the Developing World, *The Wall Street Journal*, 17 August.

Malakate, A., Andriopoulos, C. and Gotsi, M. (2007) Assessing Job Candidates' Creativity: Propositions and Future Research Directions, *Creativity and Innovation Management*, **16**(3 September): 307–316.

Markides, C. (1997) Strategic Innovation, *Sloan Management Review*, **38**(3 Spring): 9–23.

Millson, M.R. (2008/2009) Wilemon, Designing strategic innovation networks to facilitate global NPD performance, *Journal of General Management*, **34**(2 Winter): 39–56.

MTV, Madonna Full Biography, http://www.mtv.com/music/artist/madonna/artist.jhtml

Neuburger, S., Ammer, M. and Schmidt, T. (2009) *Nam June Paik: Exposition of Music, Electronic Television, Revisited*, Berlin: Buchhandlung Walther Konig GmbH & Co. KG. Abt. Verlag.

Nicols, T. (1999) *Tintoretto: Tradition and Identity*, London: Reaction Books.

O'Hagan, S. (2007) The man who sold us Damien, *The Observer*, Sunday 1 July 2007, http://www.guardian.co.uk/artanddesign/2007/jul/01/art1

Popkin, H.A.S. (2006) Just call Madonna the recycled-Material Girl, *MSNBC*, 11 October 2006. http://www.msnbc.msn.com/id/15200899/

Porter, M.E. (1996) What is Strategy?, *Harvard Business Review*, November–December.

Ready, D.A. and Conger, J.A. (2007) Make Your Company a Talent Factory, *Harvard Business Review*, **85**(6 June): 68–77.

Reckhenrich, J., Anderson, J. and Kupp, M. (2009) Art Lessons for the Global Manager, *Business Strategy Review*, **20**(1): 50–57.

Richardson, J. (2007) *Life of Picasso Vols 1–3*, Knopf.

Richardson, K.A. (2008) Managing Complex Organizations: Complexity Thinking and the Science and Art of Management, *E:CO*, **10**(2): 13–26.

Schmidt, V. (21 April 2008) Madonna goes to No. 1 for the 13th time, *The Times Online*, 21 April 2008 http://entertainment.timesonline.co.uk/tol/arts_and_entertainment/music/article3789058.ece

Schneider, E., Sischy, I., Siegel, K. and Werner Holzwarth, H. (2009) *Jeff Koons*, Köln: Taschen Verlag.

Shewan, D. (2008) Madonna Debuts Hard Candy, *Rolling Stone*, 1 May 2008.

Simons, D.J. and Chabris, C.F. (1999) Gorillas in Our Midst: Sustained Inattentional Blindness for Dynamic Events, *Perception*, **28**.

Stacey, D. (2008) Who Forgot to Pay Damien Hirst, *Bad Idea Magazine* (online), 7 November 2008.

Stachelhaus, H. (2006) *Joseph Beuys*, Neuausgabe, List Tb; Auflage.

Stepan, P. (2006) *Picasso's Collection of African and Oceanic Art: Masters of Metamorphosis*, Munich: Prestel Verlag.

Staff Writer (1992) Madonna is America's Smartest Business Woman, *Business Age*, June 1992.

Staff Writer (2005) Madonna on the dance floor, *The Sunday Telegraph*, 29 August 2005.

Staff Writer (2009) The Celebrity 100, *Forbes Magazine*, 3 June 2009.

Stockhausen, K. (1964) *Texte zu eigenen Werken, Zur Kunst Anderer, Actuelles, Aufsätze 1952–1962 zur musikalischen Praxis*, exhibition catalogue, Cologne, reprint, Paik video, p. 29.

The Times Online, http://entertainment.timesonline.co.uk/tol/arts_and_entertainment/music/article3789058.ece

Ullrich, W. (2009) Art, Price & Value – Über den Wert der Kunst, *artnet Magazin*, 28 February, http://www.artnet.de/magazine/art-price-value-uber-den-wert-der-kunst-teil-i/

van Gerstner, L. (2003) *Who Says Elephants Can't Dance?: Leading a Great Enterprise through Dramatic Change*, London: Harper Business.

Vogel, C. (2008) Bull Market for Hirst in Sotheby's 2-Day Sale, *New York Times*, 16 September 2008.

Wing, R.L. (1988) *The Art of Strategy: A New Translation of Sun Tzu's Classic The Art of War, trans*, New York: Doubleday.

Wolf, N. (2006) *I, Titian*, Munich: Prestel Verlag.

www.madonnafanclub.com

www.maverickrc.com

www.wikipedia.com

Index

Compiled by indexing Specialists (UK) Ltd